Turnberry Consulting
Development: an Approach to Strategy and Management

black dog
publishing

We know of few firms who are less keen to court publicity than Turnberry. We have operated for nearly ten years with no publicity material, no public statements and, to the disbelief of many, no website. We were convinced to collaborate on this book on the basis of its contribution to how projects work and how consulting in general can be improved.

Our first acknowledgement must be to our staff who have supported us throughout. The second is to our clients who have accepted and embraced our approach, often without limitation. Our effectiveness is almost exclusively a function of this trust.

Many people have contributed invaluably to this book, not least the Duke of Devonshire and Professor Tim Wilson, who kindly gave up their time to write the Preface and Introduction respectively. We would like to thank our clients and associates for participating in the interviews, including Nat Anderson, Martin Barnes, Peter Bazalgette, Andrew Beharrell, Alan Berrisford, Keith Dennis, Lord Doune, Douglas Erskine-Crum, David Holmes, Andrew Howard, Jim Johnston, Michael Kuhn, Joe King, Ruaraidh MacNeil, John Miller, Colin Moses, Tim del Nevo, Michael Nutt, Freda Rapson, Rod Sheard, Helen Smith, Rafael Viñoly, Chris Welch, Paul Williams and Jennifer Wood. In particular, we are grateful to the clients whose projects are described and their patience in dealing with drafts and providing images. Many practices have also kindly provided images, including Daniel Adderley, Bennetts Associates, Benson + Forsyth, Duany Plater-Zyberk & Company, David Edmonds, Glenn Howells Architects, HOK, Niall MacLoughlin Architects, Steve Morley, Pollard Thomas Edwards architects, Purcell Miller Tritton, Rafael Viñoly Architects, RMJM, Sports Turf Research Institute, and Stanton Williams. We are also grateful to Duncan McCorquodale, Nadine Monem and all the team at Black Dog Publishing.

There are others who have helped this process and many clients whose projects have not been covered. We extend our thanks to all of them, for their encouragement, collaboration and forbearance.

Jonathan Coulson and Paul Roberts
Turnberry Consulting Limited
November 2006

Contents

Preface

I was very pleased to be asked to write this Preface given my involvement with Turnberry Consulting through the redevelopment of Ascot Racecourse. As Her Majesty's Representative at Ascot and Chairman of the Ascot Board since 1997, I have seen every aspect of the redevelopment project from the original concepts, through to construction and operational readiness.

Through these phases a variety of consultants and advisors were appointed and reported or presented to the Board. Each one was recruited for a specific task that was needed at the time. It is only with hindsight that we can look back and compare the various parties involved. For more than five years, Turnberry's role was pivotal as they dealt with two issues outside our control — the grant of planning permission and the consent of our landlord, the Crown Estate. If either went awry it could have frustrated the development, and, as far as the town planning process was concerned, ostracised the local community. Not only did Turnberry execute these tasks but they provided general guidance linked to a knowledge and understanding of our racing business that was often surprising. Turnberry consistently provided an exceptional service over a sustained period of years without erring in their drive or commitment to resolve our problems.

It is no surprise that the essay by Professor Tim Wilson includes quotations that confirm Ascot's view of Turnberry and reflect my and colleagues' experiences. The case studies illustrate the extent and complexity of the other projects Turnberry has been involved with. What the essay and case studies highlight is the ability of a small company to be more effective than some companies considered amongst the largest in this particular field. My experience of working with a substantial range of consultants during the Ascot redevelopment has showed me that big does not mean best or most efficient.

Turnberry is an unusual firm whose methods are as effective as many and better than most. This book explains their approach in the context of the work they have undertaken. I would recommend this book to anybody contemplating a major project or with an interest in major projects in general.

Stoker Devonshire

The Duke of Devonshire CBE

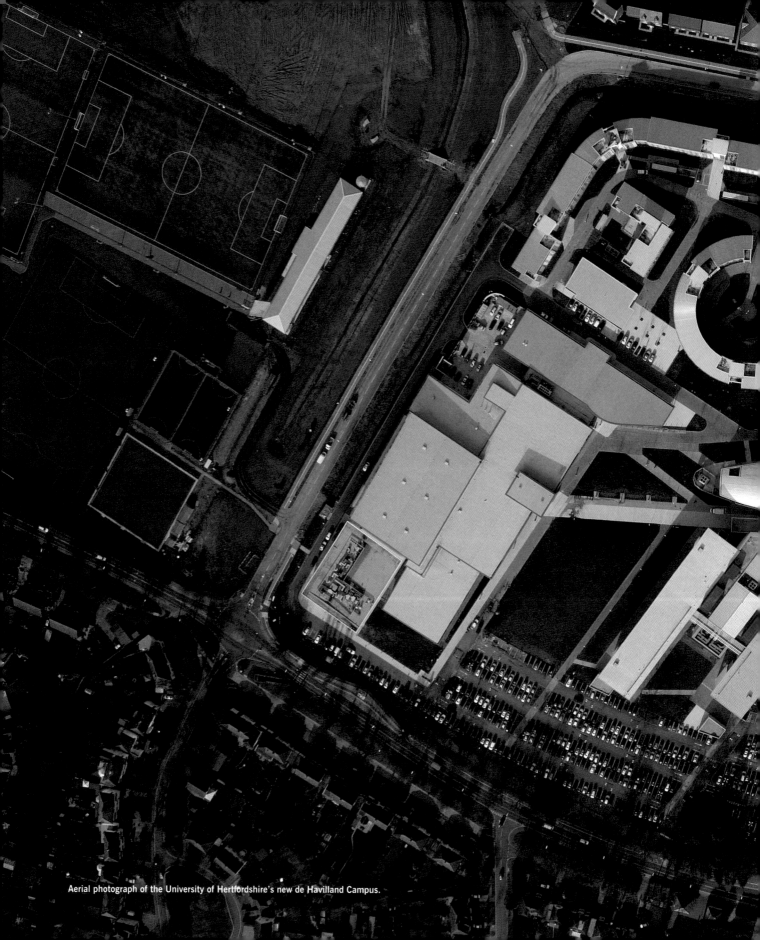

Aerial photograph of the University of Hertfordshire's new de Havilland Campus.

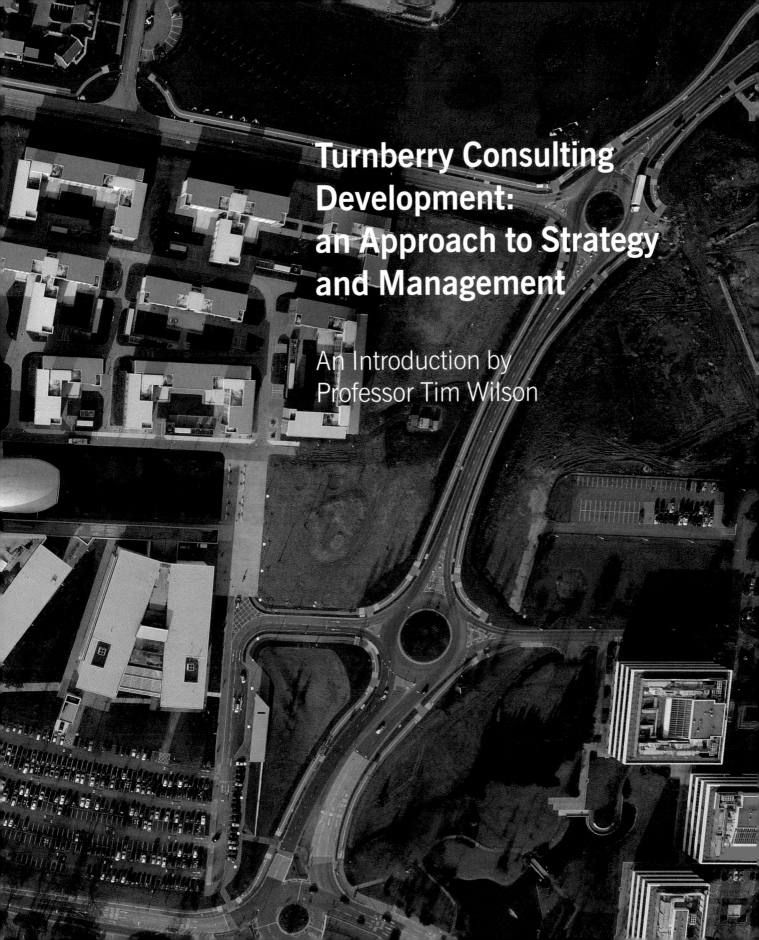

Turnberry Consulting Development: an Approach to Strategy and Management

An Introduction by
Professor Tim Wilson

It is not often that anyone is able to look back at a part of their career and objectively analyse the approach taken and decisions made. It is more unusual to be asked to do this in the context of the performance of a consultancy, to establish if there are lessons that may apply in a broader context. When I knew that Turnberry were the subject of this study, I was immediately attracted to the task.

After an early career in industry, and periods at what is now Leeds Metropolitan, Cranfield and De Montfort Universities, the phase of my career in which I had more substantial property experience came from 1992–2004 when I was Pro Vice Chancellor and Deputy Chief Executive of the University of Hertfordshire. The major and perhaps most important part of my role was the development of the University Estate. Whilst there are many factors that contribute to a successful and thriving university, the quality of the estate is often underestimated in attracting staff and students. Competition for staff and students is fundamental, and the physical and functional quality of the estate goes hand in hand with this. In my view, matching a university with its physical estate is a key element to success in a competitive higher education marketplace.

In itself, there is no trick to this and I am not unearthing here the secret of University Masterplanning. The majority of universities know that the more impressive their physical appearance, the more competitive they can be. However, given that many universities have similar access to resources, the better the strategic thought and effective delivery of an improved estate, the better competitive advantage a university can gain.

In 1992, the quality of the University Estate at Hertfordshire was very poor, which left me facing two particular challenges. The first task was to effect a change after a long period of under-investment. In many ways, a straightforward and deliverable task often provides the starting point of a significant regeneration. The second was a more difficult and more intellectual undertaking: namely to outperform the market by delivering a better solution than that of the other institutions in similar positions — a challenge which is common to nearly all forms of business and commerce. Moreover, I felt that I had around ten years to radically change the face of the University in order to best position it for future dynamics that affect the way UK universities are funded and controlled. If the University stood still, it would, in reality, be moving backward as its competitors moved forward. If I were to succeed in these tasks, I had to embrace the best practice in the sector.

In the 1990s, the University's operations spread over five principal locations, some of which were made up of multiple sites, all within Hertfordshire. This was not an efficient situation. Hatfield was the primary location and the site of the original Hatfield Technical College. Thus Hatfield was the academic and administrative centre of the University. Other important locations were the Faculty of Law's facility in St Albans next to the Law Courts, which has a logical connectivity, and the Astronomy Field Station at Bayfordbury in a rural location.

The two more difficult sites were the Business School at Hertford and the Faculty of Humanities and Education at Wall Hall in Aldenham. I will return to these two sites and the particular problems they posed in more detail when I comment on the rationalisation programme of the University Estate later in this essay. As in all business decisions, it is often appropriate to start with the more straightforward solutions that are easy to implement, having consensus across the organisation and bringing immediate impact. Frequently, these are solutions to the most acute problems. For the University of Hertfordshire, it was the creation of a new faculty building for Art and Design and the complete rationalisation of the Library facilities at Hatfield with the development of a new Learning Resources Centre (LRC) that were most urgent given the very poor quality of these facilities.

Once the LRC and the Art and Design building were underway, I now had to tackle the most difficult problems in terms of consensus, deliverability and risk — the future of Hertford and Wall Hall. As campuses, they both suffered similar problems. They were too small in terms of critical mass to accommodate appropriate facilities that could provide students with the full campus experience at remote locations. The physical fabric was an unedifying mix of under-invested 1960s system buildings alongside poorly maintained historic buildings. Even if the critical mass issue could have been resolved, the cost to bring the buildings up to an acceptable standard and maintain them thereafter would have been prohibitively expensive in the long term. I knew from the mid-1990s that Hertford and Wall Hall would not have a place in the long standing future of the University.

Faculty of Art and Design,
College Lane Campus.
Courtesy of the University
of Hertfordshire.

Learning Resource Centre,
de Havilland Campus.
Courtesy of the University
of Hertfordshire.

In 1996, the concept was devised to acquire a new site in Hatfield, as close as possible to the existing campus, shut down Hertford and Wall Hall and move 900 staff and 5,500 students to Hatfield. The logical way to do this would be to close and re-open simultaneously. This relied on the ability to lever capital out of the existing sites whilst still operational in order to forward fund the new scheme. This placed pressure on the project that made budgetary control and programming difficult. Added to this, the university calendar only allows one window of opportunity every year to undertake such a relocation, namely the start of the academic year.

The project was to be further complicated by the nature of procurement of the new campus. The academic buildings were to be directly developed by the University with the sports facilities and residences delivered through the Government's Private Finance Initiative (PFI). These two elements had to be delivered to a single Masterplan.

From conceptual planning in 1996, the scheme advanced to completion on schedule in the autumn of 2003. The budget position was not a simple capital cost, but a net cash input by the University as we had costs and sales flowing through the life of the project. In part, due to a rising residential market ahead of construction cost and inflation, the net cash input by the University was less than the budget. The capital cost of the new campus, including all costs, was eventually £120 million. The scheme started on site in 2001. The process was not without stress, moments of crisis and periods where my colleagues and I would question our decision to start. Yet at the end of the exercise, we knew it was overwhelmingly the correct course of action and a fantastic success for the University.

Since the new campus opened, I have taken on the role of Vice Chancellor and now have a different perspective of development as part of the University strategy. The success of the new de Havilland campus has led to more significant upgrading of the original College Lane Campus. In addition, the quality and efficiency of progress over the last ten years has been a major factor in attracting staff and students. I mentioned earlier that the challenge was to out-perform the market. In terms of the estate this relates to two particular areas. The first issue is to deliver best practice — schemes must be innovative and visionary.

The second is to deliver more efficiently and effectively than your competitors. Ultimately, it comes down to the capacity of the client to make decisions. In my view, decision-making is the single most important aspect of any major project. The ultimate responsibility lies with the client, but the structure of the project, availability of information, and the perceived pressure to make decisions are all material factors.

It occurred to me during the preparation of this essay that major projects, particularly bespoke projects, are often celebrated as much for their delay and cost increases as the nature of the building itself. In my lifetime, two of the most spectacular have been the Sydney Opera House and the Scottish Parliament at Holyrood. Philip Drew's 2002 book looks at the whole development process and the series of interactions that lead to the creation of the Opera House, and the resignation of Jørn Utzon from the project. More recently, Susan Bain captured the progress of the new Scottish Parliament in *Holyrood: The Inside Story* after being part of the BBC Scotland film team that had exclusive inside access to make the documentary *The Gathering Places*. I accept that every project has different characteristics. I identify the Opera House and Holyrood as they are 30 years apart and both were controversial due to the architectural appointments: the Opera House, with the resignation of Utzon in circumstances that he deemed unbearable; and Holyrood with the death of Enric Miralles and the continuation of the project by his widow, in partnership with RMJM. What I found fascinating in reading detailed accounts of these projects was that, without question, the most inexperienced people were the clients themselves. From analysis in both cases, it can be argued that the decision-making process of the client was significant in the outcome of the projects.

Over the last 30 years, all those involved in development have had the benefit of technology to assist the standardisation of processes and the removal of risk by testing or repetition. Communication and the scope for ambiguity have reduced, and globalisation has allowed for the more ready transfer of best practice. In short, it is reasonable to assume that the technical end of development has become more proficient, yet spectacular mistakes still abound.

To some extent, I excuse the development industry from this analysis as property companies and insurance pension funds retain experience from repetitive processes. Often, the most widely criticised schemes tend to be one off projects with a bespoke design in the public eye. In these circumstances, the client or client group

The new Street and Auditorium at the
de Havilland Campus. Architects: RMJM, 2003.
Courtesy and © Hufton & Crow/VIEW.

have often never previously undertaken a project of such scale or complexity. Given this context, relationships are crucial. The ability of the client to identify those core consultants to assist the direction of the project, and the ability of the consultants to establish the requirement of the client and communicate the best advice are fundamental to the success of any scheme. My hypothesis derived from my own experiences is that it is the breakdown or absence of key consultant-client relationships that have the most bearing on the success of a project.

For my part, I tend to split the consultants that work on a project into two groups — technical and strategic. The extent to which a particular discipline falls into either of these categories is a function of their impact on the project. For projects at a university, most construction disciplines would tend to fall into the technical category. Subject to proper briefings and the appointment of good quality consultants, the relative impact of a discipline such as engineering should be modest. This is not in any way to demean the importance of the role.

However, for projects at the University, construction does not tend to have a pivotal impact. By comparison, town planning issues always tend to impact on programme and, in relation to the sales of property, often have a material impact on receipts. I am always keen to interact with those consultants whose impact makes a difference and whose area of expertise can make or break a project.

With good communication and confidence on both sides, decision-making is enhanced and maximised in relation to timing, extent of information, risk and certainty of outcome. For any party inexperienced in projects and about to embark on, or be involved in, a significant project, confidence in the strategic consultants is fundamental to a successful outcome. This may seem obvious but, in my experience, it is not best practice. Optimal performance requires a clear understanding of the role and constraints as a consultant and the consultant must understand the structural, political, economic, cultural and operational imperatives of the client. Often, neither side tries to understand each other to the detriment of both.

The new Sports Social Club, de Havilland Campus. Architects: RMJM, 2002. Courtesy and © Hufton & Crow/VIEW.

There are a number of principal criteria that I apply from my experience to any consultant that is strategic to any project, over and above the usual benchmark of technical competence and track record. The particular issues that I would address are:

- Are they customer focused or company focused?

- Do they bend to your requirements or do they provide the service within the constraints of their company?

- Do they have the scale, depth and backup to deliver the task at hand?

- Who is responsible for your project day-to-day?

- Is there a breadth to their skill?

- Is there the passion, professionalism and personal commitment to solve your problem?

If a consultant can meet these criteria, and provide advice accordingly, the client has the best chance of fulfilling its role and making sound and rational decisions.

For a lay client, consultant selection and appointment is a perilous process. If you are trying to out-perform the market, public procurement processes can deliver a greater degree of mediocrity by pushing the client towards larger multi-disciplinary consultancies in an attempt to manage perceived risk. Procurement processes often fail to focus on the key factors that allow proper interaction, namely the quality of the individuals involved and the commitment of those individuals. When the size of firms is compared, there often seems to be security in a large firm over a smaller firm. However, the large firm only delivers a team of two or three people comparable to a smaller firm's team and therefore it is right to question the benefits of the larger organisation. In some circumstances, larger organisations are essential. For instance, with large construction projects, no architect without some depth to their office can produce the detailed design and working drawings required to advance a scheme; however, there are always circumstances where an architect can be selected for their concept and additions can be made to allow for delivery.

The entrance to the new Hertfordshire Sports Village
at de Havilland Campus. Architects: Austin-Smith:Lord.
Courtesy of the University of Hertfordshire.

The principal point in relation to consultant appointments on projects where you are trying to outperform the market, is that you are seeking individuals or small groups of individuals who are prepared to make a difference to what you are aiming to achieve. Over the long term, Turnberry Consulting has consistently made a difference to the University of Hertfordshire. Paul Roberts was involved in the original strategy for the development of the campus, all the planning issues for the new campus and residential sites, and some of the transactional issues to procure the academic buildings. It is certainly my view that the final solution in terms of functional and financial out-turn for the University would not have been as great with another practice.

Turnberry Consulting in itself is an unusual company, as you will find out in reading this book. It is run by two directors, Jonathan Coulson and Paul Roberts, who wholly own the business. They are selective for whom they act and selective in the fields in which they work. They almost exclusively avoid working for any organisation where finance is the principal motive for the activity. Function and operational excellence are their objectives and all their projects, as is evident from these case studies, relate to the ambition of an organisation to undertake a development which is not likely to be delivered by the market. In writing this essay, one of the issues I wanted to explore is why Turnberry has had the success it has, and why people have consistently appointed a relatively unheralded company to take on such substantial projects, often without any form of competition.

For the Earl of Moray in relation to the development of a new town, or for the University of Oxford concerning the largest development ever built by the University, or for Ascot Racecourse when building their new racecourse, to appoint Turnberry, often outside the standard competitive process, and to work with them in complete harmony for, in some cases, a decade, suggests that there is something unusual about the client/consultant relationship which may be instructive to many.

Whilst I have my own views on the success of Turnberry, I am fortunate that I can draw from a series of interviews undertaken with other clients in relation to the case studies in this book.

On the issue of customer focus, there are two things that are important. The first is an understanding of the decision-making process of any client. For example, a

University has a different decision-making process to that of a trust or a commercial/corporate entity. The availability and approval of finance and the approval of capital projects can diverge significantly. The extent of information, the quality of the information and the standardisation of capital project approval is, again, a variable issue. Any consultant who is not flexible in dealing with the particular nuances of the client decision-making will immediately start to suffer. The second issue that is fundamental to client understanding relates to the business. For instance, in working with a university, interaction with members of academic staff on a project requires a particular skill and expertise. It requires an understanding of the university culture and the pressures of the university system. Any consultant who is either not aware of or unprepared to engage in this process, is unlikely to be well regarded. Jennifer Wood, the Director of Estates at the University of Oxford, explained that:

> We use Turnberry as a catalyst… they are an exceedingly good catalyst. We set out with a strategy that Turnberry help us develop which is designed to get us to an end point where we want to be. The rest of the team that actually helps us to do this, seem to be secondary. The architects are the second people appointed — the first are Turnberry.

In order to respond to the client, it is fundamental that there is a flexibility and a desire to deal with matters which are out of the ordinary. Helen Smith, who ran the competition for the Inverness Airport Business Park, concluded that Turnberry was appointed because it was "so different that it made them interesting, and we decided to go with a wild card".

This, to some extent, reflects my earlier comment about the perception of a large firm against much smaller organisations. I am aware that for that competition the other companies bidding were global organisations, yet the panel, as evidenced by Helen Smith's comments, decided to go for what they perceived to be the 'wild card'. Smith went on to comment that:

> … the fact that Jonathan and Paul are so involved with the projects is very interesting. They have incredible expertise, other people have expertise too but I suppose one of the things that make the difference in the bigger consultancies, the managing staff might be just as experienced, but it seems to be the lesser experienced staff that are actually doing the work. Turnberry actually enjoy being hands-on. I think they really enjoy doing the work.

Jim Johnston, the Managing Director of Arlington Property Developments Ltd., who uses Turnberry in a research capacity, approached them because:

> … they have an ability to intellectualise a concept and also help us implement that concept. It is not that Turnberry are not commercial, they are commercial in a completely different way. They develop long term relationships and the income derived is not necessarily that of the speed transaction that other consultants are concerned with.

This is reinforced by Andrew Beharrell of Pollard Thomas Edwards architects (PTEa), who undertook the first Masterplan for the new settlement in the Highlands and has been involved with Turnberry on other projects. He was quite clear that "it is not just about the money — Turnberry are very clear headed about that".

Turnberry clearly have a principle that if you look after the client, then ultimately the client will look after you. That requires a substantial confidence in your ability in client selection, to know that over the long term you will be rewarded in an appropriate way. It is material in how a firm takes on a particular project and their attitude to taking on the project. There is clearly a single criterion of success that an organisation can take the long term view about financial remuneration and a client trying to judge the effectiveness of any consultant, should have careful regard to that issue. In whichever project, the crux is not how a consultant performs at interview or in the first few months in the flush of euphoria of moving a project forward. The crux is how they perform five, six, seven or eight years into the project when the budget is tight, the programme is challenging and relationships are strained.

Paul Roberts has been involved in Ascot Racecourse for nearly ten years. Over that time, Douglas Erskine-Crum has been Chief Executive of the Racecourse. He was quite clear that:

> … over the years, Paul's contribution has been much wider and much greater than just planning. In life, most things are not necessarily as complicated as we all make them out to be and Paul looks at it very simply and very rationally, and does a lot of background work to find out about it, then comes up with very simple options and solutions that most companies do not appear to be able to do.

The Business School and Faculty of Humanities and Education, de Havilland Campus. Architects: RMJM, 2003. Courtesy and © Hufton & Crow/VIEW.

Notwithstanding the obvious success of the Ascot project, especially in light of the more celebrated programmatic and budgetary difficulties of other stadia construction or redevelopment in the UK, I am sure that Ascot did have its challenges. It is unusual, and, in my experience, the exception more than the rule, for any advisor to emerge out of a long bespoke single client project with praise rather than criticism. Going back to the relationship, this may be a factor of the trust that comes from that. Jim Johnston, with whom I had personal negotiations to acquire the land for the de Havilland Campus, is interesting in his perception of Turnberry's influence.

> Once they become consultants to a certain organisation, the amount of influence they have on that client's behalf is very significant. They get into a position where they are very highly trusted and are able to manage a development strategy and implement it with a degree of authority which is unusual for a consultant to have.

This appears to be a consistent theme across all of Turnberry's clients. Chris Welch, a partner at Gardiner & Theobald who has worked with Turnberry at Ascot, Oxford and on other projects, is possibly more objective on this point than Turnberry's clients.

Lecture Theatre, de Havilland Campus.
Architects: RMJM, 2003.
Courtesy and © Hufton & Crow/VIEW.

Turnberry build fantastic relationships with clients and Turnberry
knows where they stand. I am not trying to say that Turnberry
is better than anybody else, but they understand the stakeholders
of the project, the clients and they seem able to make
difficult projects work. They know how to have fun and get
to know their clients and they have a mentality that lets them
understand the business or they can't do their job properly.

The point that Jim Johnston makes about authority is also explained by
Lord Doune, who was on the Moray Estates panel that appointed Turnberry
for the new town. He comments:

I can't conceive us doing what we are doing with anybody else
and I can't imagine us ever having the same rapport with another
company. They seed your mind with an idea in such a way
that you probably think you thought of it yourself. They then let
you reach a conclusion in your own way, in your own time.

Keith Dennis, formerly Personnel Director at Cadbury who was responsible
for the early stage development of the Masterplan at Bournville, also
identified Turnberry as extreme professionals who want to help and would
lead you gently by the hand if you did not know where you were going.

Most significant of these quotations is from Rod Sheard, the architect of Ascot,
the Principal of HOK Sport responsible for the design for Sydney Olympic
Stadium, Wembley Stadium and with Foster and Partners, the Emirates Stadium
for Arsenal and the Millennium Stadium. Rod Sheard interacted with Turnberry
during the Ascot project and worked with Paul Roberts. His perception is that:

… it takes time for people to get involved with these
buildings and understand all the nuances of them. Paul is
particularly good at that, he understood every thread of it.
It wasn't just planning, he understood the client and their
aspirations, the design team and what they wanted.

There is a consistent theme which tends to emerge from all these comments. It
is quite clear that many firms and consultants would argue that all the points I
have made in the last few paragraphs are things that they would do. From my
experience, Turnberry do set the need to understand relationships and their

clients' objectives, aspiration and business as the paramount aspect of their tasks. This requires research and thought which goes beyond the traditional approach of a client. This is my first submission as part of this essay — track record, relationships and understanding the client and its business is more fundamental to the ultimate success of the project between client and consultant than, I believe, many people perceive it to be.

The next subject is that of scale and critical mass, a determining factor in many consultant appointments. A perception exists that if someone is ill or incapacitated within a larger organisation, there is someone who can take over — there is backup, and there is strength and depth. The flipside to this is that larger organisations very often have a greater turnover of staff than smaller companies and do not tend to have the personal commitment to the project as smaller organisations do. This is not exclusively the position, but very often smaller, consultant owned businesses drive a greater aspiration towards a project than larger companies. However, scale is a legitimate matter — how do you deal with the issues of the 'small is beautiful' concept if that concept does not allow the delivery of the technical outputs needed? Clearly, this is a function to be judged by the client at an early stage. Is the appointment of the consultant going to require the availability of 20 staff at some point during the project, or is the scale of the project such that it can be constrained to a smaller number of people? My experience is that where there is a prospect of a small team of two to six staff required to effectively deliver a function, a much greater emphasis should be given to the merits of smaller companies in dealing with these issues. Turnberry is quite unusual in that some of the projects are extremely large. Some of their projects exceed half a billion pounds in likely development value yet they can cope with it with a relatively small number of people. Andrew Howard, Managing Director of Moray Estates commented that:

> Turnberry are interested in being involved in projects that make a difference. There is nothing that I would consider too big to throw at them. They are the antithesis of a big scale corporation — they are prepared to take risks, they are prepared to explore new avenues to get clients the best result which is what has proved so successful with us, and that for me is the most important thing.

The new Street and Auditorium at night, de Havilland Campus.
Courtesy and © Hufton & Crow/VIEW.

Even for a large company like Cadbury, undertaking the Masterplan of one of its largest chocolate manufacturing sites in the world, Keith Dennis "never felt anything other than complete confidence that they were doing everything that needed doing, and they did that by staying small, but dedicating time." In terms of any analysis of this issue, Chris Welch explains it very well. "Turnberry work within their capacity. I'm not sure how much bigger they can get because their business revolves around their personalities and the professional capabilities."

For me, this makes it quite clear that smaller companies can be effective, as long as they know their limitations. Returning to Rod Sheard, his experience of working for one of the world's largest firms of architects is quite incisive: "It has nothing to do with how big you are really. It has to do with who you've got, whether you've got the right team and whether you've got the right people. I don't remember a meeting at Ascot that Paul did not show up to."

Ruaraidh MacNeil has used Turnberry to deal with a number of his projects in the Highlands that he could not easily solve elsewhere. He was attracted by the fact that: "Turnberry are small enough to be flexible and effective, they call the shots within their organisation so that they can deal with unusual projects."

Much of this commentary relates to Turnberry's understanding of their client, and flexibility. A company such as Turnberry is not constrained by any corporate dogma or particular approach. When Ascot wanted to publish a history of Ascot Racecourse, they saw it as a project and passed it to Turnberry. Turnberry had never previously produced a book, but approached it with the usual research-based methodology. The book was produced and shortlisted as one of the five best illustrated sports books of the year — the only publishing project Turnberry has done. To conclude on my second point, scale is a misleading aspect. It is incorrect to say that all substantial and complex bespoke projects should be dealt with by small consultancies, or conversely by larger companies. However, in relation to the other points I have made whilst writing this, scale should not be a restricting factor. Indeed, very often it can be an extremely positive factor in providing advice to a client which is likely to help the decision-making process.

The final issue of these three points is passion of personal commitment. As a general principle, if the consultant that you employ is as passionate about the project as you are, then many of the problems will be resolved. I found a fascinating comment on this topic from Tim del Nevo, the Land Agent of the University of Oxford, who made a very honest assessment of Turnberry's sense of ownership.

> We are demanding of them and they are demanding of us... if they are engaged — they feel proprietorial. It's a two-way street... if all of your consultants were like that... you'd go home and feel exhausted every night. And they do demand and do receive high input from this end. I think if Paul were sitting here he would feel that unless we gave our best, he couldn't give his best.

Andrew Howard was 100 per cent confident that what Turnberry is looking for is the end result for the client. "In my experience, they are quite unusual in their passion for their projects." So at the end of the day the client says "Wow — that is what we wanted." Tim del Nevo went on to say they were very involved and totally engaged, whereas Chris Welch commented that "... it keeps coming back to the fact that they really care about their projects, they select projects they really want to work on".

Michael Nutt was responsible for project managing the Crossness Engines redevelopment — a charitable Trust who were unable to pay Turnberry any significant fee. It is relevant that this is a project Turnberry took on which has limited financial reward and is clearly one of the smaller commissions they have received. Notwithstanding that, Nutt said: "What we got is a team who are willing to give us more support than, frankly, the fee deserves. They put everything into it and continue to do so."

It appears that to Turnberry, the client and the acceptance of the client is the over-riding proposition. The scale of the projects is important, but their acceptance to take on a particular role ensures complete dedication to that role.

Jennifer Wood at the University of Oxford is quite clear that "… they have never let me down, that is even with them being so busy". Andrew Howard identified that "… they are looking for a solution that meets the client's needs. They are more than prepared to reinvent the wheel each time."

Their ability to be passionate and inquisitive was noted by Joe King, the New York-based track consultant for Ascot Racecourse, who highlighted a different perspective on working with Turnberry. "Turnberry was all about research, which was impressive. They were interested in looking at the total picture. They were interested in what could be, as opposed to what should be." Whilst Joe King seems to have worked on nearly every significant racetrack project across the world, he concluded that Turnberry's approach resulted in "… the most thoroughly thought through project I have ever been involved in. The interaction which Turnberry engendered through the process locks people into relationships which delivers the best outcome."

This makes it quite clear that the success of Turnberry's clients is directly connected to the fact that Turnberry really care about what they are achieving. In some ways, you get the impression that the projects are more important to Turnberry than they are to the client, although I am sure this is just a perception!

The reason I am being so emphatic about this particular point is that the driving ambition to resolve certain aspects of the de Havilland project went further than the contractual requirement that any client could have with their consultant. It required a drive and endeavour through difficult times, which in some ways can only ever be delivered by faith. A faith that you want to do a project and a faith that you want to solve all the problems. To me, being involved in consultant appointments, being advised and involved in other matters through my other roles for the University, there is never a criterion on the scoring matrix called passion or commitment. It is assumed that this is the expectation rather than the rule. If you have consultants who are passionate and committed to your project, ultimately over the long term they will deliver far greater results for you than you might otherwise expect.

My aspiration in preparing this text is not to provide a definitive client guide to consultant appointments. There is no analytical way to deal with this. What I have sought to do is explain the implications of decision-making for a client, and the importance of consulting appointments, to assist that decision-making process. From my experience with Turnberry and the experience of others that have contributed to this book, some of the more oblique issues are often forgotten or omitted by lay clients in the mechanistic world of scoring matrices, risk registers and interview appraisals. In a world of public accountability and audit trails, objective evaluation of alternatives is essential. Of those there is a need to ensure that professional advisors have the right skills and capacity to provide a service. But selecting professional advice is more than a risk management exercise; it is selecting an organisation in which you have personal trust.

That means selecting people (not an organisation) that have the same values as the client and share a passion for a project. People who will overcome obstacles by determination rather than seek to avoid blame through an audit trail. To appoint professional advisors is to entrust them with your own reputation; and that implies more than a mechanistic matrix scoring methodology assessing skills and capacity. My experience is that the University, particularly in relation to the de Havilland project, was able to deliver an output that transformed our University because of the people we employed. It is quite clear that there are other people in the UK who have employed Turnberry Consulting, and for whom Turnberry has delivered solutions, which have allowed them to achieve objectives far beyond those they could have aspired to. They do so not because it is a large company, but because it is an organisation that, unlike any other I have experienced, understands its client and its business, operates in a way and at a scale that is flexible and responsive, and encourages a passion and commitment to the projects, unparalleled in my experience.

Whether you are a client, a consultant or an advisor, there are instructive lessons here for all concerned that should be reflected on if you ever have to embark upon substantial projects.

Oxford City and its University, 2006. Courtesy David Cowlard.

University of Oxford

Dr John Radcliffe, an engraving by
Pierre Fourdrinier after Sir Godfrey Kneller, Bt.
Courtesy and © National Portrait Gallery,
London.

The Radcliffe Infirmary, its courtyard
and St Luke's Chapel, viewed from
Woodstock Road in 1908.
Courtesy and © English Heritage
National Monuments Record
Henry W Taunt Collection.

From its creation in the twelfth century, the University of Oxford has cultivated a unique reputation for excellence in education and research, and has therefore attracted the highest standard of staff and students from all over the world. In addition to its academic reputation, the University is well known for its striking historic buildings, which set a context for a variety of projects on which the University and Turnberry are working together. One such project is the Radcliffe Infirmary (RI) site for which the University is currently in the process of approving a Masterplan with the help of Turnberry Consulting.

Dr John Radcliffe bequeathed £140,000 to the University when he died in 1714, which thereafter became known as the Radcliffe Trust. Initially the gift was intended to fund the construction of a new library known as the Radcliffe Camera, but the surplus was sufficient to construct the Radcliffe Infirmary in 1770 and the Radcliffe Observatory in 1795. The site was subsequently the object of many additions over the years, with a clustering of new buildings constructed rather unsympathetically around the time the National Health Service (NHS) took responsibility for the Infirmary in 1948. In the late twentieth century it became apparent that the Infirmary's activities would be better suited to the new John Radcliffe Hospital in Headington, which encouraged the University's ambitions to acquire the site in the interest of much-needed expansion.

The Radcliffe Camera, part of the
central Bodleian Library complex.
Courtesy David Cowlard.

The Radcliffe Observatory, 2005.
Courtesy Purcell Miller Tritton.

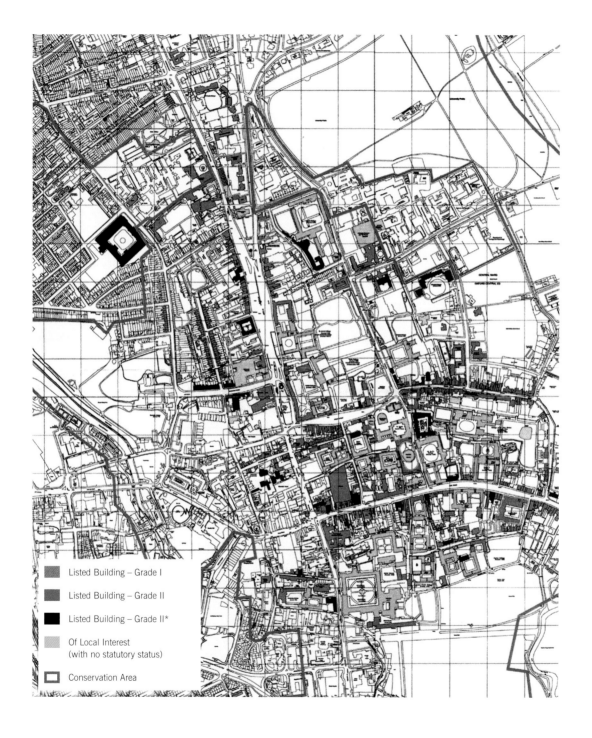

Listed Building – Grade I

Listed Building – Grade II

Listed Building – Grade II*

Of Local Interest
(with no statutory status)

Conservation Area

The Radcliffe Infirmary and its courtyard, 2005.
Courtesy David Cowlard.

Opposite: This plan illustrates the historic
context of Oxford, including all of the listed
buildings and conservation areas, 1999.
Courtesy David Edmonds.

Available real estate in the centre of Oxford has become exceedingly difficult to acquire, with the density of the existing landholdings becoming progressively more saturated. To remain competitive, the University will need to add to its functional estate over the next few decades in order to accommodate its projected growth in teaching and research activity. The University of Oxford is all too aware of the changing environment in which it must compete to maintain its reputation for excellence, particularly with its peers in the United States and the rest of the world. Therefore, it must be in a position to attract the highest calibre of staff and students, requiring the University to ensure that the standard of its facilities remains amongst the best in the world.

In 1999 Turnberry Consulting started working with the University of Oxford to produce a paper on the requirements of the University over the next 20 years, in order to demonstrate to Oxford City Council that the RI site should be reserved for the University's use in the Draft Oxford Local Plan. In preparation for this bid,

Turnberry investigated the development and growth of the University's staff, students, activities and estate in historical terms. Combining this work with extensive research of comparable universities in the USA and UK, Turnberry forecasted future growth and examined spatial models of how this could best be accommodated in decades to come. These models were put to the University and it was agreed that the historic nucleus of activities within the city centre, proximate to the Colleges, was the only long term solution that would maintain the Collegiate University. A site options analysis was undertaken and it became apparent that the RI site, as the University previously suspected, was indeed the only site worthy of consideration. This work was refined into a report in September 2000, now commonly known as the Turnberry Report. It was through this document, reviewed through the Local Plan process, that Turnberry and the University were able to convince Oxford City Council of the necessity of allocating the RI site to the University in order that it would have sufficient space to grow, and thus retain its pre-eminent status and historic value to the city, while preventing the University from expanding in an ad hoc manner on to other central city sites which might undermine the land-use balance in the City of Oxford. The second Draft Local Plan made a site-specific allocation for the RI site under policy DS66, retaining the site for the University's academic, research and administrative use. When the NHS accepted that they could not change the University allocation, it sold the site to the University on the 23 March 2003 with a leaseback option to the NHS such that they will retain occupancy until the completion of the John Radcliffe Hospital anticipated in the spring of 2007.

Once the University had overcome this most important hurdle, there were several obstacles to development for which Turnberry quickly had to provide sensitive solutions. Primary to these were the site's heritage constraints. The main listed building on the site is the 1770 Infirmary building, neighboured by the Grade II listed 1865 St Luke's Chapel, the 1858 Fountain of Triton, the gates and walls to Woodstock Road and the 1913 Outpatients building. In addition to the listed buildings on the site, there are important buildings of historical interest on adjacent sites, including the Grade I listed Observatory, the University of Oxford Press, the Royal Oak pub and Somerville College. The City of Oxford was also an early exponent of height restrictions in the interest of heritage protection, which are based on view cones from certain strategic points around the city. There is also a conservation area which wraps around the site, together with other transport and environmental concerns.

Building Construction Date

	1775
	1875
	1924
	1939
	1970

A plan showing the historical development on the Radcliffe Infirmary site, in 1970, at the peak of site coverage.
Courtesy Purcell Miller Tritton.

Due to the prominence and scale of the site, Turnberry and the University had to develop an extremely careful approach to the development for the RI site, taking into consideration the different facets of the planning issues while building a strategic team to see the project through to completion. When completed, it is estimated that it will be one of the largest ever university developments in the UK. The University's first action was to commission a full historical analysis and Conservation Plan of the site in order to address heritage concerns before appointing the design architects between January and June 2005.

Turnberry then assisted the University of Oxford through the architectural competition process, which was organised by the Royal Institute of British Architects (RIBA), with Rafael Viñoly Architects (RVA) being appointed. RVA is a critically acclaimed architectural practice based in New York City and

London, and while the practice has 170 design professionals, its principal, Rafael Viñoly, is personally involved in the design of each project. The core Masterplan Project team was then complete, with RVA as architects, Turnberry as the planning consultants and Gardiner & Theobald acting as quantity surveyors with various other consultants working on technical issues. The Masterplan Project team was then set to address the challenges of this unique project and develop clear and focused solutions for the many obstacles to development, including Oxford's heritage interests, its unique political environment, the area's conservation constraints, together with the University's complex strategic ambitions.

To approach the heritage concerns a Conservation Plan was developed by Purcell Miller Tritton Architects, based on recommendations from the historical appraisal prepared by Turnberry at the outset of the project. The contents of the Conservation Plan would inform the Masterplan and provide a framework for proposed development. The findings revealed that all three listed buildings on the site had been to some extent compromised by later (and rather insensitive) additions which would benefit from careful removal. The majority of buildings on site were built in the late nineteenth and early twentieth century and were not suitable for University purposes. Consequently it was proposed that all but the listed buildings on site would be demolished and replaced by efficient, modern buildings that would complement, rather than impede, the position of the listed structures. These principles provided the parameters for preliminary planning on the RI site.

Turnberry negotiated with Oxford City Council to reach an agreement that the University would produce a Masterplan, along with a Strategic Environment Assessment (SEA) and a residual buildings programme, that Oxford City Council will endorse after public consultation. This will establish a framework within which detailed planning applications for individual buildings could be brought forward when the University's academic need and finances allow. The purpose of the Masterplan is twofold, firstly to provide the University with a clear vision for this important site, and secondly to provide a vehicle for public engagement on the University's proposals and its subsequent approval by Oxford City Council. The public consultation suggested by Turnberry was to involve the local community in the project and inform interested parties about the University's intentions.

A concept scheme developed by Rafael
Viñoly Architects (RVA) for the Radcliffe
Infirmary site Masterplan.
Courtesy and © Rafael Viñoly Architects PC.

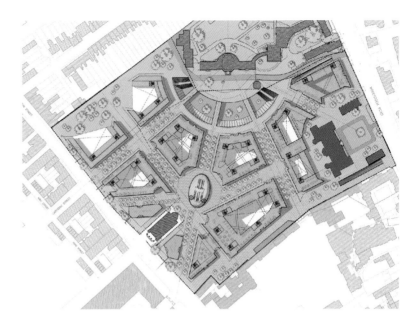

Consultation in Oxford is quite complex as the University alone has 6,000 members and many more when students, connected parties, and the University Press are considered. There is a natural interaction between consulting with the public and with the University on a private basis. From 2004–2006, the University held four internal exhibitions to explain to members of the University the original thoughts of the Masterplan appointment and the evolution and development of the Masterplan. This then widened to the relevant interest groups, statutory undertakers and members of the Oxford public. Formal public consultation is currently scheduled for early in 2007.

Whilst the RI scheme is going through the all-important consultation process, the University will set about resolving the servicing issues on the site and demolishing redundant buildings. The Radcliffe Infirmary itself will need to be wind and water tight, pending a decision on its long term future use. The first buildings are likely to be subject to detailed design in 2007, following which development will take place.

It will have been a ten year intensive process starting from the decision of the University to influence the Local Plan, through the purchase of the site, to the

Aerial view of the South Parks Science Area
with the University Parks in the distance.
Courtesy and © London Aerial Photo Library.

creation of a first building. This illustrates the inherent difficulty and range
of important issues that must be addressed in advancing schemes in places
like Oxford for the precise functional requirements of such a University.

The Radcliffe Infirmary site itself is the single largest project currently being
contemplated by the University. The University's functional estate extends
to some 490,000 square metres, which must constantly be managed to
deal with continued growth, function and suitability. This is a significant
challenge in a city such as Oxford which is constrained by a tall buildings
policy to restrict the height of development, is circled by a Green Belt
restricting outward sprawl, and has one of the highest proportion of Grade I
and Grade II* listed buildings of any city in the UK. Turnberry assisted the
University of Oxford in its review of its Estates Strategy in 2006 to provide

Internal view of the University
Museum of Natural History, designed
by architects Deane and Woodward
in the late 1850s, and located
in the South Parks area.
Courtesy Purcell Miller Tritton.

a framework for the development of the University Estate over the next 20 years. In addition, Turnberry is involved with a number of other strategic projects, one of which is a Strategic Vision for the South Parks Science Area.

The South Parks area, which includes both the Keble Triangle and the Science Area, has not met the University's desired functional, aesthetic and environmental standards for many years, to the disadvantage of those who use its facilities and to the disadvantage of science in Oxford. Consequently, in 2005, the University determined to undertake a formal estates strategy to ensure the area functions to its maximum efficiency, creating an attractive, sustainable environment that can support the academic needs of its users over the long term. The deliverability of any South Parks area development has to be sensitive to a number of issues, including transport, accessibility and the historic context. It is a large site and any development will only be optimally successful if it is considered as a single entity. Throughout the development it will continue to be operational, thus requiring activities to be decanted temporarily. The Strategic Vision is a vehicle to ensure deliverability by considering the area first holistically, and then separating it into a collection of discrete development projects, each of which are comprised of notional building envelopes and their associated public realm. The general approach is to prioritise individual projects which are readily achievable in order to create a sense of initial momentum, after which other projects can evolve naturally as and when budgets and logistics allow.

Having decided to embark on a Strategic Vision process, the University appointed a team to undertake the project at the end of 2005 and appointed Terry Farrell Architects as the architects to lead this team. Turnberry was appointed as planning consultant and liaised with the City Council to develop a bespoke planning mechanism for this large site. The first step was to consult both the City Council and English Heritage on the draft Strategic Vision and a Conservation Statement produced by conservation architects Purcell Miller Tritton. The Strategic Vision will, after approval from the University, be subject to a formal public consultation. After any changes originating from this consultation process, it is then hoped that the Vision will be endorsed by the Council, thus forming a framework within which individual applications can be brought forward in the future.

The University's historic, central Bodleian Library complex, with the Sheldonian Theatre on the right and the Clarendon Building in the left foreground, with the Bodleian New Schools Quadrangle, and the Radcliffe Camera and St Mary's Church in the distance.
Courtesy David Cowlard.

Turnberry has also been advising the University on the overall approach and the estate implications of its new library strategy, which sets out the key strategic proposals for the future development and delivery of library services. The Oxford library system has played a significant role in the cultural and intellectual life of the world for over 400 years. Alongside the British Library and the Library of Congress in Washington, the University of Oxford has arguably the most important and extensive library collections in the UK, and one of the best collections worldwide. These libraries continue to grow: stock growth is currently over 5.2 kilometres per year. The Oxford University Library Service (OULS) is a rich and diverse entity, being formally established in February 2000 as an integrated organisation managing 40 University-funded research and faculty libraries on 45 sites. The Bodleian Library, the foremost among the University's libraries, first opened to scholars in 1602, and is also of great

Internal view looking up to the Radcliffe Camera's central dome, designed by James Gibb and completed in 1749. Courtesy David Cowlard.

national and international significance, being one of the six libraries accorded legal deposit status in British legislation. It is entitled to receive a free copy of every book, periodical and newspaper published in Britain and thus acquires over 300,000 items each year. Its seven and a half million volumes occupy 188 kilometres of shelving. Other notable libraries are the Radcliffe Camera, the New Bodleian, the Sackler and the Taylorian Libraries. The combined collections of the OULS number more than 11 million printed items.

The University has recognised for a number of years that benefits might flow from the development of a more unified and rationally organised library system. There are many practical problems within the existing library buildings, with the need to upgrade and reorder the existing spaces and services, but most of the problems can only be solved by radical improvements to the physical estate.

Fundamental problems include insufficient space to accommodate the growing collection, poor quality of existing storage in terms of shelving and environmental control, a fragmented and costly estate, and difficult staff working conditions in certain buildings. A further logistical problem is the need to decant collections from buildings before major work is undertaken.

Turnberry has been working closely with the University on the various aspects of this strategy. OULS is now taking forward a 'hub and satellite concept' reorganisation, with the aim of integrating libraries and reducing the number of sites. The strategic consolidation of the libraries estate into a small number of subject 'hub' sites will be supported by smaller, specialist 'satellite' sites. This structure will be supported by a new central depository that will allow storage of the increasing collections and enable quick and efficient delivery of material to readers. The first of the hubs, the Social Science Library, is already open. Turnberry is also involved in the implementation of particular aspects of the strategy including the new depository and, also, the necessary upgrading and development of historic library buildings including the New Bodleian Library.

The most critical aspect of the library strategy is the need to keep the Bodleian Library in the historic buildings in the centre of Oxford. In order to do this, the University must redevelop the New Bodleian Library which was constructed in the 1930s to the designs of Sir Giles Gilbert Scott. The aim was to build storage for up to five million books, co-located and connected by an underground tunnel to the main, old Bodleian Library. The steel-framed 11-storey central book stack was enveloped by the Scott-designed body of the building which contained reading rooms and offices. A book conveyor and pneumatic tube system for messages allowed books to be delivered to readers in the Bodleian Library and Radcliffe Camera. This scheme was sufficient for practical purposes for many decades, but as the years have progressed increasing difficulties have arisen. The central book stack is the primary cause of these difficulties as its inflexible steel frame prevents modifications to alleviate problems. The existing mechanical and electrical systems have now passed the age when they can be realistically maintained, and the building needs to be brought up to modern standards. Yet the building's Grade II* listing means that any intervention is extremely sensitive. Turnberry completed a comprehensive historical review of the building's design and has worked

The New Bodleian Library, designed by
Sir Giles Gilbert Scott in the 1930s.
Courtesy Purcell Miller Tritton.

alongside the University, architects and conservation planners to identify the
parameters whereby a major redevelopment of the building meets the local
authority and conservation planning requirements. The vision to remove the
central stack whilst retaining and refurbishing the Scott-designed surrounding
building has so far been met with in principle support from English Heritage.
Features such as the tube system and book conveyor will be partially left in
situ. Once refurbished, the building is likely to house the University's unrivalled
Special Collections.

The University is in the process of appointing an architect to take forward the
feasibility study for the library. In order to redevelop the New Bodleian Library,
its current book stock of some three and a half million volumes must be
decanted and accommodated close to the centre of Oxford. The University has

involved Turnberry in seeking to obtain permission for a new depository at Osney Mead which will provide a home for the decanted stock from the New Bodleian Library, alongside long-term stock growth for the University Library Service. This scheme is difficult, as by its very nature, a depository is a warehouse structure where the larger the mass and volume, the more efficient the retrieval from the depository. It has no external openings which would restrict light. To place such a building close to the centre of Oxford without detriment to the skyline of Oxford is a very difficult, sensitive undertaking. It has taken much discussion with English Heritage to get to a position where they are broadly supportive of a scheme, which secures the future of the historic Bodleian complex built for Library use.

A further strand of Turnberry's work for the University relates to the continuing difficulties of attracting staff to a place like Oxford, given the problems with the housing market. Oxford as a city has a significant surplus of jobs to homes, which results in an inflated market and significant in-commuting from outside the city. Given the globalisation of academic posts and the appointment of individuals from across the world, high house prices and the unavailability of housing proximate to the University do, on occasion, result in the failure of applicants to take up posts due to the lack of suitable housing. Turnberry

Watercolour of the Wolvercote Paper Mill, painted by Leonard Squirrell in 1948. Courtesy Oxford University Press.

Aerial view of the Wolvercote site.
Courtesy and © Getmapping plc.

has assisted the University in looking at the strategy for developing solutions to this which are twofold. Oxford University Press has manufactured paper at the Wolvercote Paper Mill over the long term, a use which finally ceased in 1997. Rather than disposing of the site for commercial uses, the University has decided to develop the site for use by its own staff. This is a significant diversion of University resources to provide accommodation which will further attract high quality staff to the University. A Masterplan has been produced

Aerial view of Begbroke with a red line
marking the boundary of the site.
Courtesy and © Simmons Aerofilms.

for the site and an exhibition was held to some acclaim in Wolvercote at the end of 2005. The site itself has been in the ownership of the University Press since the nineteenth century, and in 2004 the University and the University Press considered the options for development of the site. The site presented an exceptional opportunity to create faculty housing, notwithstanding a number of technical difficulties that need to be overcome. The University has set about resolving a number of issues including ecology, transport, flood plain, archaeology and noise, whilst obtaining the confidence of the local community. By the end of 2007, a detailed scheme for the site will have been produced.

On a wider scale, the University acquired a site at Begbroke, some six miles distant from Oxford, in 1999, to gain access to the laboratories which were no longer needed by the Cookson Group. Since that time, the University has obtained planning permission for some 18,580 square metres of new development in the Green Belt at Begbroke for those activities which cannot logically be accommodated in the centre of Oxford. When the University acquired the Begbroke site, they also acquired 121 hectares of land which in 2003 was considered by Oxford County Council for release from the Green Belt. Turnberry have made representations on behalf of the University of Oxford to the South East Plan to argue for a Green Belt review of Oxford, to allow more proximate housing for easier commuting to Oxford. This could result in a significant housing allocation, part of which would accommodate University staff where they would have good road, bus, rail, cycle and pedestrian links into the centre of Oxford. Turnberry made representations on behalf of the University and together with the University will be represented at the Examination in Public at the South East Plan in 2007.

These projects illustrate the over-arching and interlocking strategy the University of Oxford must pursue in order to provide the best and most suitable facilities for all areas of activity. In the last few years, Turnberry have assisted the University with the majority of those strategic property issues that will shape the University's future. What is apparent is that a deep understanding of the functional needs of the University and a research-based approach is the only way to effectively advance projects of a world-class nature and in a difficult environment.

The Chocolate Factory at Bournville. Courtesy Cadbury Trebor Bassett

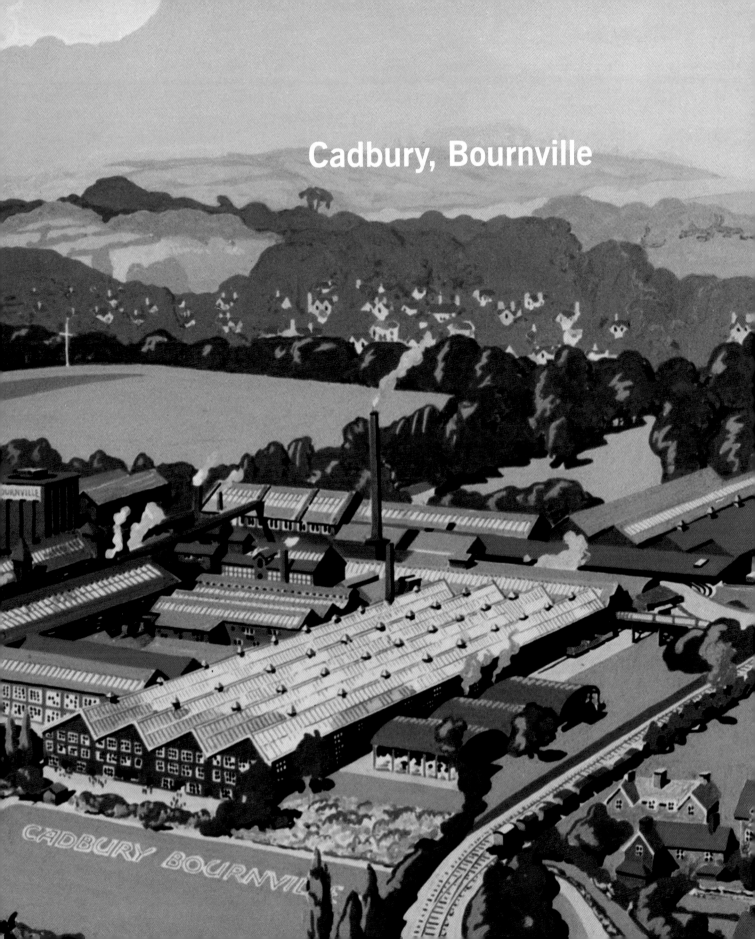

Cadbury, Bournville

John Cadbury.
Courtesy Cadbury Trebor Bassett.

George Cadbury.
Courtesy Cadbury Trebor Bassett.

In 1831, John Cadbury rented a warehouse in Crooked Street, Birmingham, to roast and grind cocoa, founding what was to be one of the UK's most popular and distinctive confectioners. By 1878, the Cadbury Brothers had outgrown its Birmingham base and Richard and George Cadbury set out to develop a more comprehensive manufacturing base on a newly acquired six hectare estate in Bournbrook (later to be renamed Bournville). The Cadbury Brothers, being devout Quakers, envisioned the construction of a 'model factory' exemplary in both its efficient functional layout and in its attention to the welfare of its workers. Therefore, alongside the well-planned factory, the company provided social and recreational facilities in the form of a playground for women and sports facilities for men to enrich the lives of its employees.

The factory expanded dramatically from 1880 to 1899, with a seven-fold increase in floor space, tripling the overall area. In 1886, the 'A' Block was built, along with the No. 1 Lodge in 1888, both of which have since been demolished. In 1884, the first railway siding was built into the site, followed by the construction of the 1889 Director's Office, now known as the No. 1 Lodge. In 1895, Cadbury purchased the Bournbrook Hall Estate, which comprised land to the north, west and south of the original site, including the Bournbrook Hall Manor. The land was designated for a girls' recreational ground, a men's recreational ground and an area for factory development. The original walled kitchen garden behind the Bournbrook Hall was used for teaching, gardening and producing various plants for the factory. The built environment on the site was also shaped by the company policy such that men and women were separated; besides separate grounds, there were also separate workrooms and dining rooms and the entrances were positioned to ensure that gender segregation was maintained in all activities.

By the 1900s, the Bournville site was known as the "Factory in a Garden" and renowned for being an innovative and well-equipped factory in a pleasant environment.

Promotional posters for Cadbury's
vision of a model factory at Bournville.
Courtesy Cadbury Trebor Bassett.

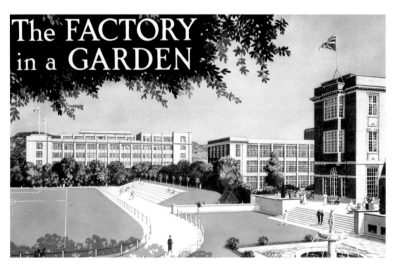

The Girls' Baths in operation
during the 1930s.
Courtesy Cadbury Trebor Bassett.

The turn of the century saw more development with a second railway line
constructed to the east of the site in 1901, and in 1902 the men's pavilion
was given to Cadbury as a gift celebrating Edward VII's coronation. The
Girls' Baths was constructed in 1904, notable for both its architecture and
innovation, and distinctive as the largest covered baths in Birmingham and
the Birmingham district at the time. After the demolition of Bournbrook
Hall in 1907, the firm re-landscaped the girls' recreational grounds and
built new greenhouses in the walled garden. Between 1920 and 1937
there was another surge in development with manufacturing floor space
increasing by 100 per cent. The new buildings were designed with the
application of gravitational flow, so that materials began their journey
from the top of the building downwards in a one-way production line.

Poster commemorating the
centenary of the Cadbury firm,
showing the growth of the
factories from the original
Bridge Street factory to
Bournville in 1931.
Courtesy Cadbury Trebor Bassett.

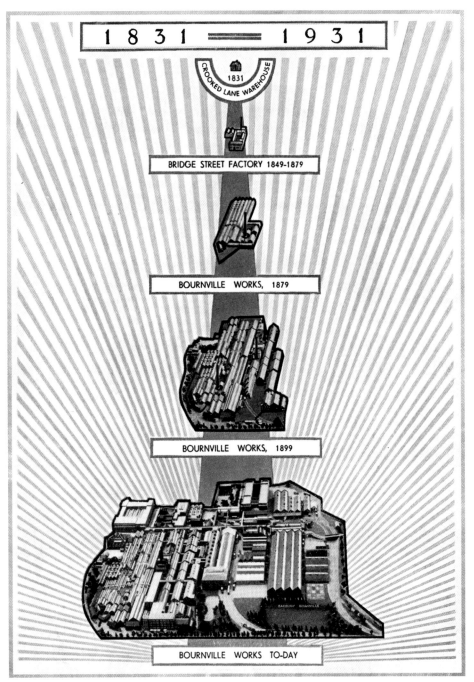

Historic Ordnance Survey Maps showing the development of the Bournville factory; top to bottom, left to right: 1884, 1904, 1921 and 2002. Courtesy and © Ordnance Survey Maps.

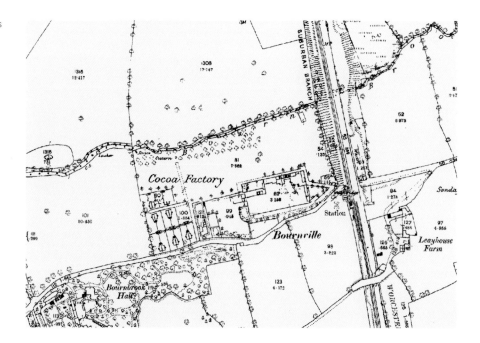

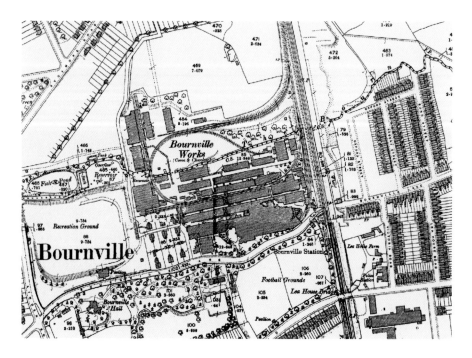

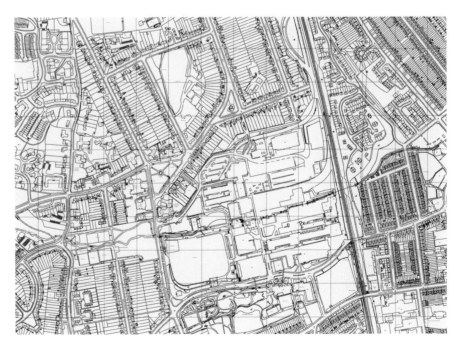

Historic photographs showing the construction of the Dining Block and the same views following completion. Courtesy Cadbury Trebor Bassett.

In the inter-war period, the Dining Block was constructed for the employees and was, under the design guidance of architect James Miller, completed in 1926. It contained extensive dining facilities, as well as a concert hall, a library and reading room, doctor and dentist surgeries, a photographic dark room and various club rooms. The building was in fact constructed in phases during this period, with the design subjected to much review and refinement throughout.

Following a lull in construction during the Second World War, Cadbury resumed development between 1956 and 1959 with the erection of the Franklin Block

Lunchtime at the Dining Block.
Courtesy Cadbury Trebor Bassett.

to decant offices out of prime production areas. The Girls' Baths received a partial face-lift in 1977, and in the year following the railway line was removed.

In the 1980s, the Bournville site underwent a period of demolition with the removal of many of the older buildings. This period saw a change in the approach from construction of new buildings to intensification of plant in existing buildings and the rationalisation of the site in general. Cadbury closed the Girls' Baths in 1982 after surveys indicated that necessary structural works and refurbishment were too expensive to implement. Thereafter, the only substantial new development was the construction and opening of the Cadbury World Visitor Centre in 1990.

Aerial view of the Bournville
factory site, 2001.
Courtesy and © Simmons Aerofilms.

Today the Bournville site is an important economic centre for the Birmingham area, with Cadbury Trebor Bassett (CTB) standing as one of the largest manufacturing based employers in the region, with around 2,000 staff (including seasonality) employed in a manufacturing capacity on the site, and in excess of 1,000 staff within an office-based environment. Taking account of this employment and CTB's significant turnover, the company has a major economic presence in both the Birmingham area and the UK in general. Further, Cadbury World is a significant tourist attraction with annual visitor numbers totalling in excess of 500,000.

In the late 1990s and the turn of the century, following a period of significant corporate restructuring and review, CTB identified the Bournville site as a centre of excellence for manufacturing in the UK. The site produces around half of all finished CTB product distributed worldwide. Considering that CTB holds an approximate 30 per cent share in all confectionery sales in the UK, Bournville appears even more economically significant to both the regional and national economy. Notwithstanding the significance of the Bournville site,

Existing Activities 2004

- Manufacturing and Distribution
- Conservation Area
- Office Administration
- Access/Circulation/Parking
- Sport and Recreation
- Cadbury World and other Visitor Facilities
- Recreation Building
- Unused/Not in Cadbury Control

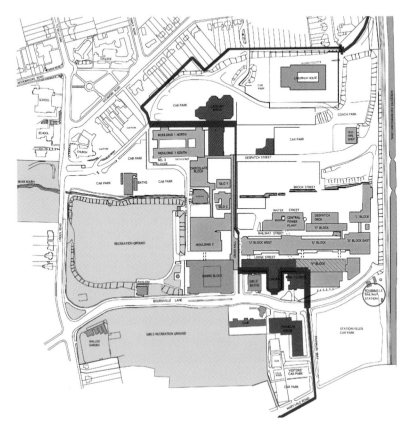

Masterplan by architects Stanton Williams showing the key activities on the Bournville factory complex, produced as part of the Strategic Plan. Courtesy Stanton Williams.

the company also recognised at this time that it had some longstanding problems that required attention if Bournville was to prosper as a manufacturing site over the long term. Firstly, manufacturing activity at Bournville was located in sub-optimal buildings, with height restrictions, traffic flow difficulties and storage problems impeding distribution. There was also a conflict between vehicular and pedestrian movements, which created challenges in terms of site safety. Further, there was an over-supply of office accommodation, but an under-supply of office accommodation of an acceptable standard, providing no consistent standard for office space across the company. Dining facilities were also considered to need upgrading for both staff and visitors. Finally, many of the heritage buildings were at risk of neglect.

It was therefore determined that a plan for redevelopment of the Bournville site was of utmost importance to sit alongside the company strategy of manufacturing excellence at Bournville. Turnberry Consulting was appointed to work with Cadbury to define a Strategic Plan to provide a context for all future decisions on capital expenditure affecting the physical estate at Bournville. The plan also identified a strategy for preserving and enhancing the heritage buildings as well as producing a specific strategy to address the long-term needs for office and dining facilities on the site. Crucial to all of this was the need to ensure a flexible environment within which the current and future requirement for manufacturing and distribution can be achieved.

As part of this Strategic Plan, Guiding Principles were formulated, beginning with a commitment to allow manufacturing to develop on the Bournville site without being fettered by its historical legacy. It was also determined that there should be an alignment between the image and reputation that the company wishes to portray and their practical and physical presence on the ground. It was concluded that capital expenditure should be targeted to help change the attitude and approach to the management of the buildings and infrastructure at Bournville. Above all, any plan for future development must be flexible to change.

With the Strategic Plan and a set of Guiding Principles in place, Turnberry worked with CTB and the consultant team to create a Masterplan comprising of six key elements, which collectively make up the Bournville Estate. Manufacturing and distribution accounts for the major part of the Masterplan and four separate proposals were set out under this heading, the first of which stresses the important preliminary project of constructing a new boiler house along with the demolition of the existing boiler house and associated brick stacks. The project has subsequently been implemented with planning permission obtained by Turnberry in 2003. The second proposal concerned the demolition of under-utilised and obsolete manufacturing buildings to, over time, enable the potential for further manufacturing development on the site.

Phases 1 and 2 of the Masterplan.
Courtesy RMJM.

Internal view of the refurbished
Grade II listed Girls' Baths.
Courtesy David Cowlard.

View of the refurbished Grade II listed
Girls' Baths from Bournville Lane.
Courtesy David Cowlard.

View in 2006 of the new Boiler House.
Courtesy David Cowlard.

The Grade II listed Sports Pavilion, 2006.
Courtesy David Cowlard.

This aspect of the plan has also now been largely implemented with the demolition of a number of redundant buildings to the rear of the site between 2001 and 2003. The final two manufacturing proposals essentially look to the phased expansion of activity to the rear of the site. These proposals have no fixed time attached to them and will only be implemented as and when demand and a business case arises.

The preservation and enhancement of the historic estate represents another large part of the Masterplan. There are three listed buildings within the Estate, beginning with the Grade II Girls' Baths which had been in a poor state of repair for many years and in need of significant renovation and refurbishment. Working with Turnberry, CTB enlisted the help of conservation architects, Rodney Melville and Partners, and other specialist advisors to prepare a scheme aimed at restoring the Girls' Baths and ensuring the building could be put to a functional future use as the phased implementation of the Masterplan continued. Turnberry obtained all necessary consents from Birmingham City Council and the repair and refurbishment works were completed in 2005. The total project included a new roof structure and cover, as well as substantial structural repairs to the clock tower and elevations of the building. The next phase of works, which is still only at a conceptual design stage, is to consider the internal alteration and fit out of the building for Cadbury use.

The Grade II listed Walled Garden is also in need of repair and lies unoccupied. This is one of the last remaining elements of the original Bournbrook Hall estate. In 2001, Listed Building Consent was granted to CTB to demolish the dilapidated former greenhouse structures which were attached to the Walled Garden, and this work has now been completed. Consideration is now being given to the future use that Cadbury wish to put this site to.

Finally, the Grade II listed Sports Pavilion is currently used for a variety of sports related activities, and unlike the other listed buildings on the site, is in a reasonable state of repair. The Masterplan proposes to continue to maintain the building and allow the continuation of its current use.

Laburnum House
Linden Block
Dining Block
Franklin House

Location of the Linden, Franklin, Laburnum and Dining Blocks. These buildings were all considered as part of the review of office accommodation. Courtesy Stanton Williams.

At the time the Masterplan was conceived, the Bournville office-based staff numbered 1,200. A strategy for office accommodation was therefore a key element of the process. Refurbishment options for each of the existing offices on-site were considered. These have included a survey of the Linden Block, the Dining Block, Franklin House and Laburnum House. The key objectives in the analysis of these options was the development of a single high quality office facility capable of accommodating 600 workstations over the long term. In the interest of avoiding conflict between heritage-based objectives in the Masterplan, the strategic team determined that the utilisation of existing property assets was preferable. As a result of these and other stated objectives, it was concluded that a comprehensive refurbishment of the Dining Block was the best option to achieve CTB's aims for a single office and administration building, with the least amount of impact on the historic Estate.

THE NEW DINING HALL BUILDINGS.
Western elevation, from the Men's Recreation Grounds.

THE NEW DINING HALL BUILDINGS.
South Elevation, from Bournville Lane.

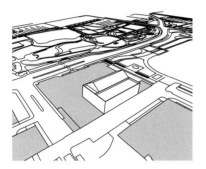

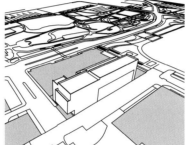

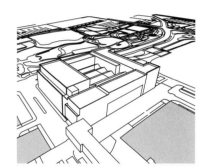

Top: Artist's impressions of the initial concept design for the Dining Block, which subsequently changed significantly following input from the Cadbury Board. Courtesy Cadbury Trebor Bassett.

Architect's illustrations showing the three phases in which the Dining Block was constructed. Courtesy Stanton Williams.

In view of the historic status of the building, a substantial amount of research was undertaken to understand in detail the design philosophy and functionality of the building to inform the development of a scheme for refurbishment. The Dining Block was in fact originally developed over a series of phases and, curiously, had no significant main entrance, but rather a series of functional access points orientated towards the factory. The building as originally constructed can be described as significant 'pavilions' to the east and west, but with a more plain in-fill zone between. It was this area that was proposed for demolition by the appointed architects, Stanton Williams, with the overall objective being to enhance the setting and connectivity of the building overall, and also to increase the amount of usable floorspace suitable for a modern day office environment. This significant alteration allowed for the creation of a new main entrance and atrium to the south.

The proposal includes the refurbishment of the top two floors as offices, with the ground floor a mix of offices, reception, meeting space and a break-out cafe area. The design also allowed for the refurbishment of the existing theatre at a later stage, possibly to provide meeting, seminar and conference facilities for the business. The creation of a new south facade is aimed at enhancing the quality and presence of the building within the setting of the Conservation Area. Finally, the partial removal of the west terrace allows for the separation of the Cadbury staff from the public north-south axis, drawing natural daylight into the dining spaces and creating an externally landscaped private eating area.

This was a significant development proposal in planning terms and attracted a significant level of local interest. Time was of the essence as Cadbury wanted planning permission and Conservation Area Consent in place as quickly as possible, in order that detailed design development did not have to proceed at risk. Turnberry therefore devised a planning strategy that included presentations to the Council at Councillor and Officer level, and also to the local community. An exhibition and brochure were also prepared to maximise the flow of information. Ultimately, the process was successful with permission granted in three months and issued in late October 2003.

It was determined on the back of these proposals that the Linden Block could be demolished, and the lease for the occupation of Franklin House relinquished in due course. Stanton Williams as the appointed architects were responsible for the design set out above. As with the Girls' Baths — although clearly on a different scale — the project was split into two phases. The first phase, which was completed in spring 2006, essentially included all of the demolition, new build and structural alterations. The second phase commenced in October 2006, and this will comprise all of the fit out necessary to allow the building to be ready for occupation in 2007.

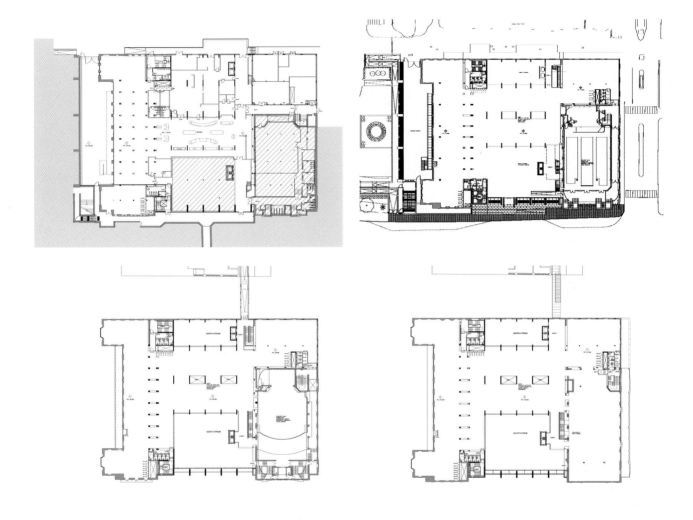

Floor plans of the approved Dining Block
refurbishment scheme, as designed by Stanton
Williams. Left to right, top to bottom: lower
ground floor, ground floor, first floor, second floor.
Courtesy Stanton Williams.

Artist's impression of the Dining Block's new atrium. Courtesy Hay Davidson.

Artist's impression of the completed Dining Block scheme, illustrating in particular the re-routed pedestrian walkway to the west of the building. Courtesy Stanton Williams.

In terms of access, circulation and parking, in time the Masterplan proposes to close the existing access point and develop a new point of entrance to the Estate on Bournville Lane at the site of the demolished Linden Block to be used for manufacturing and distribution related traffic only. In line with the Masterplan, pedestrian movement has already been re-routed such that a pedestrian link now runs along Bournville Lane and across the front of the refurbished Dining Block before cutting across the Conservation Area along the boundary of the Men's Recreation Ground, providing pedestrians with a safer and more pleasing route through the Bournville site. Additionally, CTB is now preparing a management plan in order to prioritise and allocate parking spaces, while encouraging staff to use alternative methods of sustainable transport.

Historically, the provision of sport and recreation facilities was paramount to the Cadbury ethos at Bournville, but much has changed since that time, not the least of which is the demand for high level indoor rather than outdoor facilities. CTB is currently responsible for the maintenance of these sports areas, and the Masterplan seeks to ensure efficient and effective management of these facilities to meet the needs of the business moving forward.

The proposed south facade
of the Dining Block.
Courtesy Hay Davidson.

For Cadbury World, the Masterplan seeks to support the opportunity for continued growth of this activity as and when the need can be justified.

The rebuilding of Bournville was driven by manufacturing requirement for the long-term. Once this decision was made, an overall strategic plan for the Estate was necessary to make the all-important first steps. The Masterplan addresses the significance and potential of the site in economic development terms within the local, city and regional context, while remaining sensitive to the heritage value of the Bournville Estate, the buildings and the surrounding Bournville village. Taken as a whole, these changes represent a comprehensive and reasoned approach to redevelopment on the Bournville site, allowing CTB to achieve its commercial goals while enriching the cultural quality of the Bournville area.

The Queen's colt Alexander wins the 1956 Royal Hunt Cup at
Ascot Racecourse ridden by Harry Carr. Courtesy and © Hulton Archive.

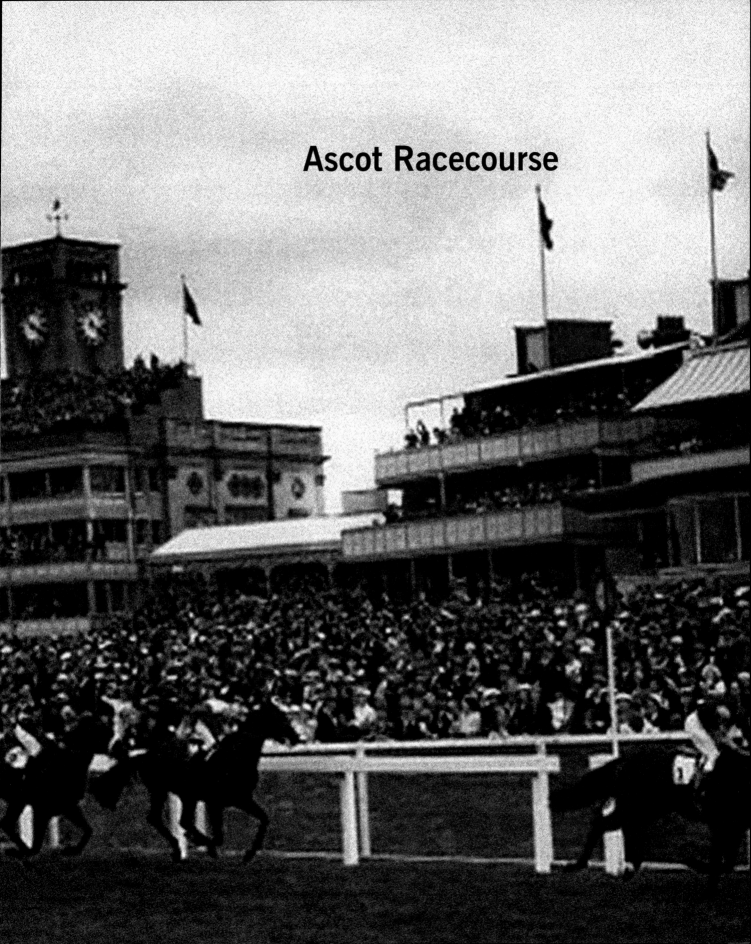

Ascot Racecourse

When the first horses raced at Ascot on 11 August 1711, the course comprised a single round heat. Queen Anne, a consummate racing enthusiast and the founder of Ascot racecourse, offered a £100 prize to the winner of the fixture's major event two days later, the Queen's Plate. The Crown Estate retains ownership of the land, but since a 1913 Act of Parliament the Ascot Authority has been responsible for the management of the venue's activities with a mandate to promote and maintain Ascot as a successful racecourse. The Ascot Authority comprises three trustees, the most senior of which is Her Majesty's Representative, currently the Duke of Devonshire. The Ascot Authority is ultimately under the direction of Her Majesty the Queen and will continue to operate in this manner, though it has reorganised its underlying businesses into a new corporate structure with great success.

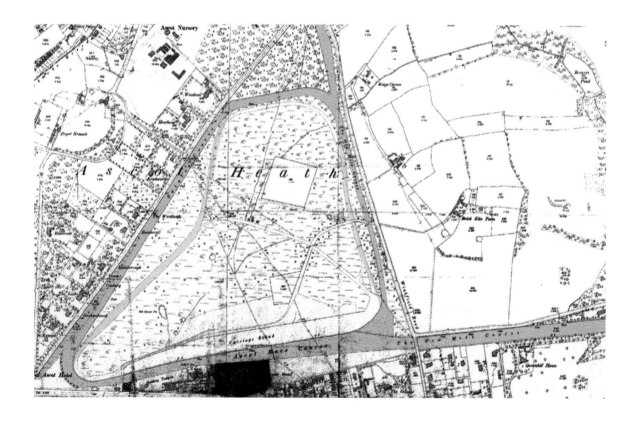

There have been many changes at Ascot since that first round heat, with continual development on the site. In the eighteenth century, makeshift wooden stands were erected to accommodate increasing interest in the races. Even the Royal Stand was wooden at this time and moved around to provide different views for the royal family. In 1793, the first permanent stand was built, named the Slingsby Stand in honour of its builder and owner. Around 1753, the Old Mile was constructed and bush and harrowing was undertaken to improve the quality of the turf. The course saw further improvements in 1825, when the track from the Paddock Bend to Kennel Gate was straightened, and again in 1861 when the Straight Mile was widened and realigned. In 1887, the Straight Mile was moved eight metres to the north in order to provide more room for viewing stands and the bend joining the round course to the Old Mile was

These images were presented to The Queen during Royal Ascot 2002. They show the changing alignment of the track in the eighteenth and nineteenth centuries (opposite), and the changing layout of the grandstands and associated buildings in 1910, 1960 and 2000 (right, top to bottom). Courtesy Daniel Adderley.

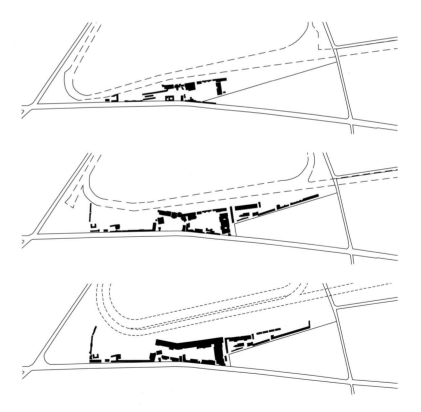

Saddling up the horses for the 1839
Gold Cup at Ascot.
Courtesy and © Mary Evans
Picture Library.

made more gradual. The first permanent building for the Royal Stand was built in 1807, only to be replaced by the decadent Nash building in 1822. Victorian grandstands were constructed in 1839, complemented by a variety of new stands to accommodate the Jockey Club and the growing racing industry. At the same time the Slingsby Stand was demolished to make room for extended enclosures, and luncheon rooms were provided for the increasingly large middle-class crowds. In 1902, New Royal Enclosure stands were built, and the Five Shilling Stand (now the Silver Ring) was constructed in 1908 to accommodate those racegoers who could not afford grandstand rates.

Great Western Railways poster,
1897, for Ascot Races.
Courtesy Ascot Racecourse Ltd.

Between 1901 and 1930, several bars and luncheon rooms sprang up in the Silver Ring, Grandstand enclosures and Paddock in order to service the growing crowds visiting Ascot each year. 1948 saw significant track improvements with the creation of the new Straight Mile, which was accompanied by extensive track work concluded in time for the 1955 meeting. The Duke of Norfolk replaced the old grandstand in the early 1960s, while at the same time a new Royal Enclosure took the place of its Edwardian predecessor.

Ascot has emerged from its long history as one of the premier racecourses in the world. The King George VI and Queen Elizabeth Stakes is not only the UK's top Group 1 race, but Ascot also boasts nine Group 1 races, ten Group 2 races and eight Group 3 races. The course also offers more prize money on the flat than any other British course. One measure of a racecourse's merit is the International Classification, which provides rankings agreed by a panel of handicappers from the major racing countries. In particular, the runners of the King George VI and Queen Elizabeth Stakes are often some of the highest ranking horses.

The racecourse has important economic and social implications for the village of Ascot, attracting 80,000 racegoers on Gold Cup days (and around 60,000 on other days) with a turnover of £40 million per annum. While Ascot Racecourse only employs around 100 direct staff, its purchasing power in the local area is significant and the indirect effect of its racing activities attracts some 750,000 people to the area every year, with important benefits to local business and services. There is also a myriad of non-raceday activities that occur on the site, including a mixture of large conferences, small meetings and formal lunches. There are a number of other groups who use Ascot for their activities, including the Ascot United Football team, the Ascot Locomotive Society, the Royal Ascot Golf Club, the Royal Ascot Cricket Club, Driving for the Disabled, Ascot Nursery School and the Cadets.

It is clear from this varied and vast list of interested parties and community members that Ascot Racecourse lies at the very heart of the village of Ascot and the British Equine Industry itself. Therefore it is of the utmost importance that it retains its pre-eminent status in the racing world for the benefit, not only of the local area, but of the national and international racing community as a whole.

Raoul Dufy's *Ascot*, 1930.
Courtesy and © ADAGP, Paris and DACS,
London, 2006.

Ascot racecourse was looking tired in the late twentieth century, with 40-year-old facilities and a track that had a series of crossings, and, as racing became ever increasingly intercontinental, it became clear that in order for Ascot to remain competitive it had to provide a world-class racecourse and facilities to match the quality of its racing. This suggested that wholesale redevelopment of the site was necessary to rectify some of Ascot's longstanding shortcomings in order to ensure the racecourse's capacity to compete for customers in a

Ascot Racecourse in 1936
as seen from the Heath.
Courtesy and © Hutton Archive.

growing and sophisticated sporting events market. A major investment was proposed to modernise and improve the quality of existing facilities, providing a sustainable development to meet twenty-first century expectations of a premier racecourse and maintain Ascot's competitive global position, while securing the requisite recreational and economic benefits for the local community.

There were a number of longstanding problems with the racecourse that needed to be addressed in order for Ascot to meet its objectives. Primarily, the racing surfaces suffered from no fewer than six crossings, the worst of which intersected the Straight Mile at Winkfield Road. Anticlockwise from that point, there were five more crossings infringing on the track: the Golf Course crossing, one at Holloway's Gate, another at Swinley Bottom, the Kennel Gate crossing and finally a crossing linking the car park to the inside of the track. The effects of these road and footway crossings severely undermined the quality of the track, with the racing surface inconsistent as a result of alterations and additions over the years. There was also poor drainage infrastructure for the racecourse, causing some racedays to be cancelled due to waterlogging. The surface of the tracks themselves was severely outdated and failed to make use of the considerable developments in turf technology over recent years. The stands and main facilities, now some 40 years old or older, were deteriorating and becoming increasingly difficult and costly to maintain. They also had a disjointed appearance as a result of their evolution over time and failed to provide sufficient space for servicing requirements. Ascot's arrival experience was rather unimpressive as well, failing to provide the visual impact expected from a world-class racecourse. Additional to these shortcomings, access to the racecourse was poor, with too few people able to access the Pre-Parade Ring, the Parade Ring and the Winner's Enclosure, while narrow pedestrian routes between the main centres of activity restricted pedestrian flow, causing congestion, especially on peak days. This worsening situation made redevelopment imperative to ensure Ascot's status as a premier racecourse. Indeed, any decline in its success would have devastating consequences for the economic viability of the local areas, the British Equine Industry and the community activities that take place on the site.

The Royal Procession at Royal Ascot.
Courtesy David Cowlard.

Despite this critical situation, there were some unique constraints to planning on the Ascot site, as the proposed redevelopment involved construction on a Green Belt site, and affected a designated Wildlife Heritage site and an area of Special Landscape Importance. The site also contains two listed buildings, the Steward's House (known as the Turnstiles and Offices) and the Totalisator Building, which demanded sensitive planning strategy. There were also the local concerns to be considered relating to the scale of development, interruption to recreation on the Heath, community access and activities to the site and issues relating to transportation and traffic.

After an intensive selection process, the strategic team evolved to have HOK's Rod Sheard as architect, Martin Barnes as client advisor, Chris Welch from Gardiner & Theobald as quantity surveyor, PriceWaterhouseCoopers as funding consultants, Joe King from New York and the Sports Turf Research Institute as turf consultants, and Turnberry Consulting as property and planning consultants. In addition, Turnberry provided general advice and comparative analysis for the new racecourse.

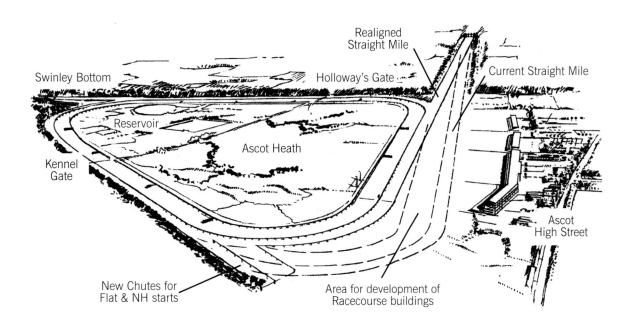

Ascot Racecourse

Swinley Bottom

Reservoir

Kennel
Gate

Ascot Heath

Holloway's Gate

Realigned
Straight Mile

Current Straight Mile

Ascot
High Street

New Chutes for
Flat & NH starts

Area for development of
Racecourse buildings

Public consultation drawing illustrating
the realignment of the Straight Mile.
Courtesy Daniel Adderley.

One of the first exercises of the strategic team was to undertake a fact-finding mission, visiting premier racecourses around the world to get a sense of the state and standard of international horseracing while aligning aims and objectives for the redevelopment. In 2000, a feasibility study of six options for the redevelopment was undertaken to determine the best course of action in addressing the congestion and operational constraints of the main facilities, while remaining sensitive to the special planning requirements of the Ascot site. The first option was the maintenance and refurbishment of existing buildings, which was quickly rejected because it did not address the need to improve facilities or account for long-term deterioration. A second option was to renovate and extend the existing buildings to the rear of the stands, but this too was discarded because it would do little to improve crowd circulation or access to facilities. Another option was considered, which involved rebuilding the existing buildings and relocating the racetrack 18 metres to the north, but it was determined that this course of action would fail to provide the necessary space to meet Ascot's objectives. The fourth possibility considered was to rebuild the existing facilities, relocate the racetrack 18 metres to the north and relocate Ascot's High Street southward.

83

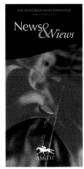
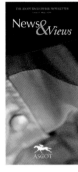

News & Views, the public information newsletter distributed to the local community throughout the planning process. Courtesy Ascot Racecourse Ltd.

However, it became apparent that, while this would create the necessary space, it would also have constituted a massive upheaval of a road re-alignment, along with associated environmental and planning complications. Another option was contemplated whereby Ascot could build new facilities, including permanent structures to accommodate maximum crowd numbers as well as relocate the racetrack 42 metres to the north. It was concluded that this option was not only too expensive, but also provided for crowd volume only seen on five days of the year. Finally, a sixth option was considered that saw the reconstruction of existing facilities, including high-quality temporary structures and permanent facilities, and the re-alignment of the track 42 metres to the north. It was eventually determined that this last option was the only one that could provide Ascot with the space it required and was the most practical and flexible approach to meeting the Racecourse's objectives.

The scheme did not require the relocation of the High Street and had the necessary limited impact on the Green Belt while at the same time provided an opportunity for improving the track. Ascot and its planning team were convinced that this last option offered the best solution to requirements for greater space, circulation of spectators and the need for better covered facilities. The two listed buildings on the site were to be renovated so as to return them to their original form. The scheme also provided for track work improvements, including the removal of road crossings by means of two underpasses (at Winkfield Road and Holloway's Gate) and revolutionary turf technology developed specifically for Ascot, called the Moveable Turf Crossing (MTC), whereby the turf would retract at the Kennel Gate crossing to reveal the road underneath. There were also provisions for a new pond on the site, adjacent to the existing pond, to provide for greater irrigation and drainage capacity on the Heath. In addition to these proposed alterations and additions, the scheme included a plan to relocate the Royal Ascot Golf Course and the Ascot Locomotive Society to Ascot Farm.

The process began with extensive pre-application and ongoing consultation with the planning authority, statutory consultees, the parish council, local groups and members of the public, including posting of mail shots to the local area and the regular printing and distribution of the public information newsletter *News & Views.*

Aerial view of Ascot Racecourse
during the Diamond Meeting, 2000.
Courtesy and © Simmons Aerofilms.

Aerial view of Ascot Racecourse
during Royal Ascot, 2006.
Courtesy Ascot Racecourse Ltd.

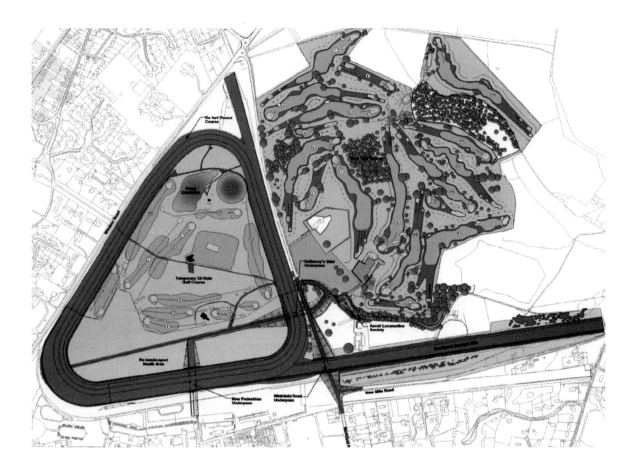

Underpass schemes and relocation
of Royal Ascot Golf Club.
Courtesy HOK Sport.

The main planning applications for the first phase of development were submitted
in September 2001, and following the planning authority's adoption of the
Planning Brief in May 2002, further planning applications and requests for
Listed Building Consent were submitted in November 2003. These applications
were contingent on the need for prior track realignment because the new
grandstand was to be built on the site of the old Straight Mile.

The six initial planning applications submitted by Turnberry on behalf of Ascot
related to an application for track realignment and associated works, which
included the corresponding realignment of the track, extension of the pedestrian
underpass between the Grandstand and the Heath and the reorganisation of the

The new Grandstand that opened at Royal Ascot 2006, viewed from the 3 furlong post on the Straight Mile. Courtesy David Cowlard.

spectator area to the north of the track. The second application related to the underpass and new junction at Winkfield Road. This was justified by pointing out that the then-existing track along Holloway's Gate and Winkfield Road was of poor standard, damaging the racing surface, race activity, vehicular activity, pedestrian activity, highway safety and the servicing of activities like the Royal Golf Course. The third planning application dealt with the formation of the new pond. The fourth and fifth applications were submitted to seek permission for the relocation of the Royal Ascot Golf Course and Clubhouse to Ascot Farm, to secure a future for the Golf Course on an improved site and to create greater access to Ascot Heath for the local community, while the latter provided a new Golf Clubhouse while remaining sensitive to the surrounding vernacular agricultural buildings. The proposal also included provisions for a

golf practice area and a practice putting green. Similarly, a sixth application
was made to relocate the facilities for the Ascot Locomotive Society on
the grounds that it occupied the site of the proposed Straight Mile. Along
with each of these proposals, Ascot and Turnberry included Environmental
and Planning Statements to supplement and clarify the proposals.

The planning application for the main facility provided for the comprehensive
redevelopment of the racecourse facilities to provide a Grandstand, conference
and banqueting facilities, servicing facilities, Parade Ring and associated
works. The scheme also included plans for alterations to the former listed
Tote Building (including demolition of the East Wing and Troy Bar) in order
to provide stables, saddling boxes, vet, wash-down, farriers and hospitality
rooms on the upper floors. Additionally, alterations to the listed Turnstiles and
Office Building were proposed (including the removal of the West Wing and
redundant turnstiles) to provide for hospitality accommodation. Again, the
Environmental Statement submitted along with the application examined all
of the environmental issues surrounding the proposal and the impact of the
scheme as a whole. The planning process resulted in the approval of more
than 20 planning applications, including consents for listed buildings, five
legal agreements (four planning-related and one concerning highways) and
numerous licenses from the Department of Environment, Food and Rural Affairs
for the requisite habitat plans providing for the protected species in the area.

The Grandstand was to be set further north and east of the previous structure,
thereby improving Ascot's arrival experience, pedestrian movement and
increasing operational efficiency. The new Grandstand included the main
racing facilities, the stepped viewing boxes, clubs, restaurants and facilities
for medical and security services. The Parade Ring was to be moved to a
central location between the Grandstand and Ascot's High Street, and the
saddling boxes were then to return to the old stables (the listed Totalisator
Building) through a comprehensive restoration of that structure. The building
on the Silver Ring was to be replaced by a grass terrace and the future Silver
Ring was to be dependent on temporary structures with some necessary
permanent infrastructure for power and services. The gross floor area of
the new facilities were to be comparable to that of the previous structure,
while built to a much higher architectural and aesthetic standard.

Artist's illustrations of the operation
of the Moveable Turf Crossing (MTC)
at Kennel Gate.
Courtesy Daniel Adderley.

To address the quality of the racetrack itself, Turnberry solicited the help of international turf specialist Joe King, together with researchers at Sports Turf Research Institute (STRI). A great deal of research went into blends of grasses that were variously historic and contemporary, with more than 20 test plots deployed in Newmarket. The Moveable Turf Crossing (MTC) employed at the Kennel Gate crossing was developed at STRI specifically for Ascot, representing a major racecourse innovation. Two underpasses addressed the crossings at Winkfield Road and Holloway's Gate, reducing the number of crossings to three, though it is the eventual aim of the Racecourse to replace all crossings either with MTC or with underpasses. The Straight Mile was repositioned so that the One-Mile start remained in the same place but the rest of the course pivots to the north, positioning the round flat course and the jumping course at the winning post about 40 metres north from where they were previously. The essential nature of Ascot as a racecourse is preserved, despite these radical changes. For example, the rise from the Golden Gates to the finish, and a similar gradient from Swinley Bottom remain relatively unaffected, retaining Ascot's unique racing character in the international racing culture.

Ascot, with the help of Turnberry, was very careful to address issues of local concern and consult interested parties throughout the entire planning and development process. In July 2002, Ascot held public meetings to explain the proposed scheme, and during the time of applications Ascot set up a local consultative group under the chairmanship of David Lunn, the Chief Executive of the Royal Borough of Windsor and Maidenhead. The consultative group consisted of representatives of voluntary and residents' associations, and other interested parties in the Ascot area. Indeed, around 46 different groups were consulted throughout the development process about their own particular requirements relating to the Ascot site. The group met once every three months for a period of eight years to identify areas of local opportunity and concern, while at the same time using the meetings as a mechanism for judging the appropriateness of the plans as they emerged.

Green Belt boundaries were created after Ascot was built, so while the fixtures of the Racecourse do not constitute Green Belt land, anything outside those boundaries would impact on the Green Belt and could therefore only be developed in very special circumstances. As a result of its repositioning, the new Racecourse was to be partially on Green Belt land and therefore required a sensitive planning approach on behalf of

The Moveable Turf Crossing (MTC), showing the tray sliding into position and a detail of its operational mechanism. Courtesy Sports Turf Research Institute.

Ascot and Turnberry. In a Planning Statement submitted to planning authorities in February 2004, Ascot set out the very special circumstances they believed were sufficient to justify the grant of planning permission on the Green Belt. The contents of this statement referred to Ascot's world-class racing status and the necessity of redevelopment in order to maintain and extend that reputation, while also pointing to the fact that its continued success is vital to the promotion of international horseracing and thoroughbred breeding, the British Equine Industry, as well as the regional and local economy. The document concluded that there was no viable option to meet the needs of the racecourse other than limited development on the Green Belt, and with some requests for clarification, the case was successful.

As a result of this argument, permission was granted without the need for a public inquiry and Ascot was allowed to commence development in 2004 with the racecourse re-opening for Royal Ascot in 2006. The efficiency of the planning process was a function of the rigorous early analysis and extensive consultation that allowed the scheme to evolve in harmony with the local community, rather than in conflict.

The new Grandstand viewed from the Parade Ring. Courtesy David Cowlard.

The Horse Walk from the
Pre-Parade to the Parade Ring.
Courtesy David Cowlard.

The entire process included the submission of more than 100 documents
and productions, including environmental statements, planning statements
and numerous supplementary documents like the Ascot Heath Ecological
Management Plan, the Golf Course Ecological Management Plan, the
Green Travel Plan and the Raceday Travel Plan. These undertakings and
others helped to ensure that the Ascot redevelopment was approached in a
sustainable and responsible manner, to the benefit of all. Indeed, the level
of research regarding the redevelopment and historical importance of Ascot
was so high, and the contents so thorough, that the resulting compendium
became the basis for the book *Ascot: the History* written by Sean Magee
with Sally Aird (of Turnberry), published by Methuen Press to coincide
with the Queen's Golden Jubilee in 2002. Additionally, resulting from the
quality of historical research undertaken by Turnberry, Ascot commissioned

Internal view of the new Grandstand.
Courtesy David Cowlard.

the company to perform a wholesale renovation and reorganisation of the
Ascot Archives to ensure the longevity of the materials stored therein.

The redevelopment of Ascot opened to many plaudits in the summer of
2006. Only 608 days had elapsed since the racecourse closed, with minimal
disruption to racing activities and the surrounding community, and maximum
benefits for greater efficiency, aesthetic merit and welfare of the local area. The
redevelopment saw the improvement of the visual amenity of the area through
replacing existing buildings with those of a much higher design quality, improving
the views of the gateway from the Western Approach and the retention and
enhancement of listed buildings and their settings. The aesthetic environment
is further enhanced in the relationship between the Green Belt and the street
scene resulting from opening up views of open land from Ascot's High Street.

The new Grandstand, Royal Ascot, 2006. Courtesy David Cowlard.

Racegoers looking down to the Parade Ring from the fourth floor balcony, Royal Ascot, 2006. Courtesy David Cowlard.

The new Grandstand, Royal Ascot, 2006.
Courtesy David Cowlard.

The redevelopment also saw the improvement of Ascot Heath's ecological health through the introduction of a new pond, thereby diversifying the existing habitat for the benefit of the protected species in the area. The Ascot Heath Management Plan and the Golf Course Management Plan ensures a higher level of ecological management at Ascot for future generations, along with improved sustainable transport through the Green Travel Plan and Raceday Travel Plans. The traffic and transportation situation also benefited from the new development, with improved traffic flow on Winkfield Road resulting from the construction of two underpasses, and improved highway safety along the High Street resulting from articulate road alterations. The conflict of uses of the Heath was resolved through the relocation of the Royal Ascot Golf Club and the Ascot Locomotive Society, along with various other groups who have been re-accommodated where necessary. Beyond the construction of (arguably) one of the best racecourses in the world, the new Ascot Racecourse vastly improves the provision of sport, recreation and leisure activities for the community while greatly improving the economic and employment potential for the local area. The project represents a wholly sustainable development that has ensured the continued status of the Racecourse for the benefit of Ascot's future generations.

External view of the recently opened Centre for Health Sciences.
Courtesy Ewen Weatherspoon Photography.

Centre for Health Sciences
Inverness

In the late 1990s the local enterprise company Highlands and Islands Enterprise-Inverness and East Highlands (HIE-IEH) succeeded in attracting a diabetes-focused medical devices company by the name of Inverness Medical to move to Inverness. It was located adjacent to the Raigmore General Hospital, which is an acute hospital as well as one of the largest general hospitals in the UK. As a result of its success, Inverness Medical was later taken over by an American pharmaceutical company, Johnson & Johnson and renamed Lifescan.

During the creation of Lifescan, HIE-IEH contemplated developing a medically-based research building proximate to both the Hospital and Lifescan in order to both take advantage of the intellectual environment of the area, and resolve some of the very significant training difficulties which occurred for post-graduate nursing, dental and general medical training in the Highlands, all of which were provided in substandard facilities. HIE-IEH's objective was to consolidate a number of life science and medical based activities into a single building, called the Inverness Centre for Health Sciences, thereby providing enhanced

Aerial view of the site of the Centre for Health Sciences showing the proximity to the Raigmore Hospital and Lifescan. Courtesy and © John Paul Photography.

Visualisation of the Centre for Health
Sciences at Inverness produced by the
concept architect, Bennetts Associates.
Courtesy Bennetts Associates.

facilities for the various potential users, while creating an environment of
intellectual and clinical cross-pollination. These and other plans were in part
contingent on Lifescan's performing significant research activity in the new
development, so when the company decided to locate all their research facilities
in a separate building close to their existing factory, HIE-IEH was facing the
potential collapse of the entire scheme. The decision of Lifescan to consolidate
its research in Inverness was a vote of confidence in the area, but left the
Centre for Health Sciences short of its principal tenant. All this occurred in the
absence of a university in the Highlands and Islands. The UHI Millennium
Institute was still in its fledgling stage and HIE-IEH had to be bold if it was
to take advantage of the limited research activity that existed in the area.

Turnberry Consulting was appointed to salvage the Centre for Health Sciences
project in the face of widespread scepticism on the part of most of the interested
parties regarding the ability of the HIE-IEH, or indeed anyone, to develop a
successful scheme that was deliverable and affordable. Turnberry identified
one of the principal stumbling blocks to a unified commitment and enthusiasm
toward a new scheme as the lack of any vision or pictorial representation of how
the development could be delivered. At the same time there was an opportunity
to meet the final application programme for the European Regional Development
Fund (ERDF) to try and lever some financial support to progress the project.

The atrium of the recently opened
Centre for Health Sciences.
Courtesy Ewen Weatherspoon
Photography.

Taken as a whole, the planning environment suggested that if HIE-IEH took a risk and developed a scheme, more certainty for the development would follow, as well as a better cost plan and a cohesive goal for the interested parties. This decision needed significant faith and confidence from HIE-IEH as at this time they were to embark on spending significant sums of money with no guarantee of success.

Turnberry organised an architectural competition on behalf of HIE-IEH through which Bennetts Associates were appointed, and wasting no time commenced the briefing and development design to ensure planning permission could be granted, in view of planned ERDF applications. This period of increased activity and building momentum inspired confidence in everyone concerned, aligning aims and objectives and creating a more positive attitude to the potential success of the new development.

The atrium (above) and external view
(below) of the recently opened
Centre for Health Sciences.
Courtesy Ewen Weatherspoon Photography.

Though morale was lifted, the difficult issue of budget remained. The involvement of the NHS could only occur with Scottish Executive approval in Edinburgh, which was a very complex process of ratifying a business plan featuring more significant revenue input than other facilities in the Highlands. The project was likely to result in a significant increased cost of provision, but promised dramatically enhanced facilities, bringing a world class medical centre to the Highlands. It was, and still is, the position of Turnberry and the HIE-IEH that there should be no reason why anybody training in medical or dentistry related activities in the Highlands should be offered, or accept, any more modest facilities than the rest of the UK. For this and other reasons, the scheme was pushed forward and HIE-IEH invited Dr Mac Armstrong, the Chief Medical Officer for Scotland, to chair the working group charged with the task of identifying solutions for the scheme as it developed. This led to an extremely difficult and interrelated group of issues that have been intensively and consistently managed by Turnberry in conjunction with HIE-IEH.

The constant enthusiasm of HIE-IEH and the desire to progress this project was a fundamental factor in ensuring matters proceeded smoothly. HIE-IEH took significant risks in terms of committing revenue to the scheme to make sure it stayed on track and in July 2005 the legal agreements were signed which led to works starting on site in the autumn of 2005. Phase 1 completed in late 2006, with Phase 2 due to follow quickly. Recently, it has been decided to proceed with Phase 3 of the development, which would be a joint venture between the University of Highlands and Islands Millennium Institute, Lifescan and the NHS. This phase is intended to unify the diabetes-related departments within the Hospital and bring them together with commercial research activity at Lifescan.

The Centre for Health Sciences is a study in effort over inertia. The decision of HIE-IEH to exploit the intellectual capital of the region was greater than the bureaucracy of the decision-making process. Without the decision to press on and design the scheme, consensus over the building would never have occurred.

The northern waters of Loch Ness, with Bona Lighthouse located
on the west side of the entrance to the Caledonian Canal.
Courtesy and © Tom Baker Photography

Bona Lighthouse
Loch Ness

Bona Lighthouse was built around 1815 as part of the construction of the Caledonian Canal. The idea for a canal crossing the Highlands began in the late eighteenth century due to the depressed state of the local economy, and to allow the British Navy safe passage by avoiding the Pentland Firth. The need to stop the flow of the population emigrating was becoming a serious issue. One avenue was to develop the fishing industry by building new harbours linked by new roads and a canal. This became the Caledonian Canal. Two engineers shared the task, William Jessop and Thomas Telford, although it is almost universally the latter that is credited with the work. Jessop was also responsible for the Grand Junction, now part of the Grand Union Canal, and worked alongside Telford on the Ellesmere Canal. Telford was born in Westerkirk in Scotland in 1757 and became famous for his engineering work through the UK, which included churches, roads, canals, aqueducts, docks and bridges.

Work began on the Canal in 1802, and it opened 20 years later in October 1822. The scale of the work was immense and employed large numbers of the local population. One of the major features is 'Neptune's Staircase' — the series of locks at Banavie. When it was opened, the Canal was hailed as a great achievement and within 15 years over 500 ships were passing through each year.

Bona Lighthouse, located at the top of Loch Ness beside the entrance to the Caledonian Canal.
Courtesy and © John Paul Photography.

Bona Lighthouse, derelict and empty
in 2005.
Courtesy and © John Paul Photography.

As part of this construction work, the Bona Narrows was widened and
dredged and is now 85 metres wide. Adjacent, Bona Lighthouse was built.
Bona Lighthouse was once the smallest manned lighthouse in the UK. It
is significant that it was manned, not just for its size, but also as an inland
lighthouse. The Lighthouse originally marked the exit of Loch Ness by a light
from the bay window at the front. As it only had to aid traffic leaving the Loch,
the light only emanated from this front window, creating an unusual layout
for a lighthouse. Traffic travelling down the Caledonian Canal to the Loch
would not have seen a light. The building is now obsolete as a lighthouse as
navigation lights are attached to a separate mast. With the end of its useful
life as a lighthouse, the building fell into disrepair and now stands empty.

In 2005 Jacobite Cruises, the principal cruise ship operators on Loch Ness, were
interested in acquiring a new site in order to consolidate its operations under the
stewardship of new owner Freda Rapson. Rapson's aim was both to build the
quality of visitor experience suitable for Loch Ness while providing more variation
in the types of cruises available to customers. At present the cruises operate from
two locations, the Clansman Hotel and the Tomnahurich Bridge, both of which
have longstanding problems that represent obstacles to delivering the best possible
cruise experience. The Clansman Hotel, for example, has inadequate facilities and

Phase 1
Phase 2
Phase 3

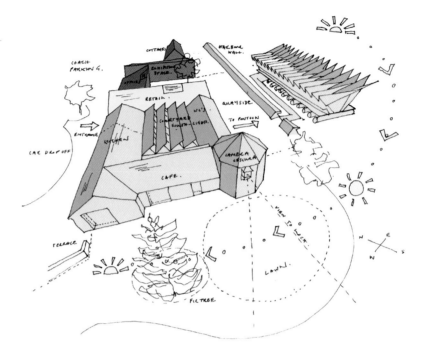

A sketch of the new scheme for
Bona Lighthouse, giving it new life
as a visitor centre.
Courtesy Niall McLaughlin Architects.

no long-term security of tenure. Similarly, the Tomnahurich Bridge is too far from the
Loch to produce short, attractive cruises, and is impoverished in terms of facilities
with little car parking and poor access. Beyond these and other shortcomings, the
company's jetty is in modest condition with significant future maintenance costs.

Jacobite Cruises decided to develop a new departure and arrival site, but found
there was very little flat, accessible and developable land around Loch Ness
on which planning permission might be granted. The Bona Lighthouse was
eventually identified as a preferred site because of its optimum location in relation
to existing buildings, and benefited from the fact that it was already zoned for
leisure development. The Lighthouse is located at the edge of Loch Ness at
the north end, close to the settlement of Lochend. It is owned by the British
Waterways Board (BWB), but has been disused for some time and is in a state
of serious decline, even though the Lighthouse was listed by Historic Scotland
as a building of regional importance in 1971. The main building has three
rooms on the ground floor with a small kitchen. A staircase leads up to the first
floor room, which is located in the main element of the working lighthouse, the
building's octagonal tower. There is also a garage to the east side of the tower,

Concept design for a new jetty at
Bona Lighthouse on the edge of the
Caledonian Canal and Loch Ness.
Courtesy Niall McLaughlin Architects.

and a walled garden to the rear. It is the aim of Jacobite cruises to refurbish
this underused building, restoring it to its original splendour while providing
some adjacent visitor facilities to enhance the experience of the site.

In view of planning for these and other aims, Jacobite Cruises decided to contemplate
a side-by-side arrangement with BWB and Dochfour Estate, who own the access
and further land required to achieve the necessary scale of development.

Once there was some interest in the principle of development by the landowners,
Turnberry Consulting undertook a feasibility study of the proposed site, taking
current operations into consideration and developing a cost plan for the
scheme's progression. Through a short competition organised by Turnberry,
Niall McLaughlin Architects emerged as the redevelopment designers, producing
a plan for the refurbishment of the Lighthouse, along with the creation of
ticketing, cafe and retail facilities. The local residents have been consulted at
various junctures in the scheme's development, which has proved an important
indicator for potential areas of concern. The project is currently in the process
of being reviewed in light of local consultation, after which a planning application
is set to be made by Jacobite Cruises with the help of Turnberry. The aim is
to open Bona in 2008 celebrating the Thomas Telford original creation.

Aerial photograph of the area between Inverness and Nairn, known locally as the A96 Corridor. Courtesy and © Getmapping plc.

Tornagrain
a Planned Town
for the Highlands

With a growing population and a potential economic boom, Scotland's Highlands and Islands needed to devise a long-term plan to accommodate the region's mounting residential needs. One of the main objectives of Highlands and Islands Enterprise (HIE), the local enterprise company, is to unlock potential and help create a strong, diverse and sustainable community through an increase in population across the region (especially in the most remote areas) and an increasing number of jobs in a wider span of economic activities.

Inverness and parts of the Highlands have together undergone a much-needed positive transformation over the last 30 years. The population of the wider Inverness City area has grown by 34 per cent during this period, which equates to an extra 30,000 people in Inverness and Nairn since the 1970s. The Highland Council expect this to continue over the next 30 years. Household growth would occur even without population growth as households get smaller. If population growth is added, then The Highland Council expect a need for a significant number of new homes over this period.

Because of physical constraints preventing the growth of Inverness to the north, west and south, The Highland Council has identified the A96 Corridor, including East Inverness and Nairn, as the main growth area for jobs and homes. The A96 Corridor is ideally suited for this role given its excellent transport links and existing employment allocations.

The expectation for growth is encapsulated in the National Planning Framework for Scotland, published in 2004, which sets out a spatial development perspective for the whole of Scotland to the year 2025. The Framework is not a blueprint for the precise location and scale of specific development, but it is a material consideration in framing planning policy and is taken into account by the Scottish Executive and its agencies in the formulation of policy and spending decisions. The Framework recognises that Inverness is the main administrative, medical, retail and leisure centre for the Highlands.

Inverness

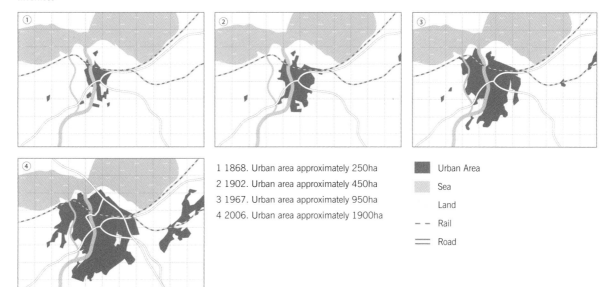

1 1868. Urban area approximately 250ha
2 1902. Urban area approximately 450ha
3 1967. Urban area approximately 950ha
4 2006. Urban area approximately 1900ha

Urban Area
Sea
Land
Rail
Road

Nairn

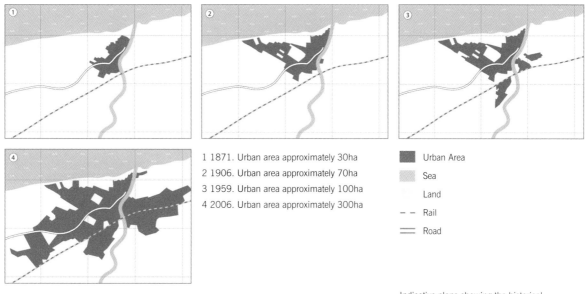

1 1871. Urban area approximately 30ha
2 1906. Urban area approximately 70ha
3 1959. Urban area approximately 100ha
4 2006. Urban area approximately 300ha

Urban Area
Sea
Land
Rail
Road

Indicative plans showing the historical growth of Inverness and Nairn from the nineteenth century to 2006.
Courtesy Purcell Miller Tritton.

The Framework also recognises the strategic importance of the A96 Corridor as it states that although Inverness's economic base remains relatively narrow, "Inverness and the Inner Moray Firth is an economic development zone with considerable potential. To the east of the city, the A96 Corridor and the Airport offer opportunities for future expansion."

At a regional level, the Highland Structure Plan expands on why the A96 Corridor offers a sustainable option for meeting housing needs in the region, stating that "the A96 Corridor provides an option of linking new housing development to business opportunities associated with the airport and rail link to Inverness and Nairn". The Plan recognises the physical constraints, particularly of Inverness and the transport opportunities offered within the A96 Corridor, making this area the most appropriate location to achieve long-term planned, sustainable growth.

At a local level, the Inverness Local Plan, which was adopted in March 2006, and the Inverness City Vision, 2003, endorse The Highland Council's view of the strategic importance of the Corridor in terms of housing provision for the region. The two documents acknowledge the suitability of the A96 Corridor as the optimum location for longer-term development post-2011.

The two Local Plans for Inverness and for Nairn covering the Corridor prioritise the development of established housing and community land allocations situated within existing settlements. These areas have sufficient capacity to meet expected needs until 2011.

The Council has applied a corresponding policy within the A96 Corridor which sets a strict presumption against piecemeal and premature development during that period. The main exception to this is the proposal to develop a business park and associated activity on land adjacent to Inverness Airport and the A96 itself. The location for this is broadly equidistant between Nairn and Inverness. The proposal is being promoted through a public-private joint venture consortium which includes Highlands and Island Airports, HIE-Inverness and East Highlands (HIE-IEH), and Moray Estates.

The Estate is in fact one of the most substantial landowners in the A96 Corridor, having owned the Castle Stuart Estate since 1562, and which now extends to over 2,500 hectares. The prospect of responding to The Highland Council's work on the A96 Corridor and seeking to identify possible development opportunities for its land in the Corridor was therefore an extremely exciting one for the Estate.

Notwithstanding this, the Estate's first discussions with the Council on the principles of growth were not met with a full understanding of what the proposals for change could hold for the region. Since that time, and working alongside its principal advisors, Turnberry Consulting, the Estate has embarked on a rigorous programme of research and analysis in order to identify the optimal scheme that could be achieved from development of its land in the Corridor.

Early in the process, Turnberry's commission was to advise the Estate on the discussions and submission made to the Council and its initial advisors FG Burnett, on the first level analysis undertaken to identify how best to deliver the forecasted population growth for the A96 Corridor. The Stage 1 'Proof of Concept' phase was completed by FG Burnett in mid-2005. This looked in broad terms at an appropriate settlement hierarchy for the Corridor sufficient to accommodate the proposed population expansion. In understanding this analysis, FG Burnett devised a series of options for growth which it sought to debate with statutory bodies, key stakeholders and the wider public through a consultation format described as 'Collaboration for Success'. Underpinning these options from the outset was the Council's vision of a 'Triple Helix' — that is, a strategy for growth in the area linked by road, rail and pedestrian corridors.

Alongside this work, the initial studies undertaken by the Estate quickly led it to conclude that its land was best suited to the promotion of a large, new settlement located broadly centrally within the Corridor and adjacent to the Airport and proposed business park. This land is located close to the existing small settlement of Tornagrain, and this soon became the working title for the proposal.

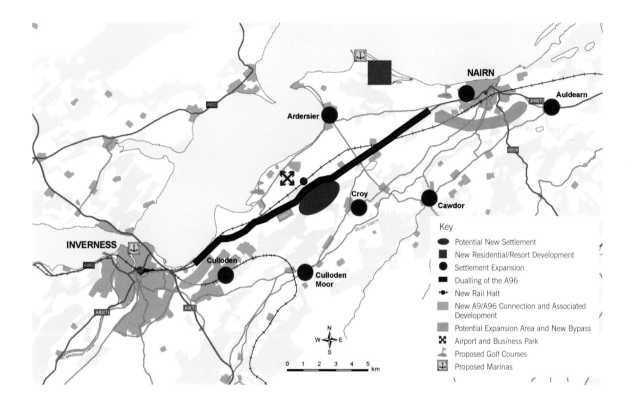

Key
- Potential New Settlement
- New Residential/Resort Development
- Settlement Expansion
- Dualling of the A96
- New Rail Halt
- New A9/A96 Connection and Associated Development
- Potential Expansion Area and New Bypass
- Airport and Business Park
- Proposed Golf Courses
- Proposed Marinas

The Highland Council A96
Corridor Masterplan.
Courtesy The Highland Council.

The initial project team, appointed by the Estate for the development of Tornagrain, saw Turnberry Consulting as the lead advisors, Pollard Thomas Edwards architects (PTEa) as architects and masterplanners, Alan Baxter Associates as consulting engineers, Whitelaw Turkington as landscape architects and Fulcrum Consulting as engineers. With a cohesive team having agreed on a strategy and developed options for the site, the time was then right to lay down some conceptual groundwork for potential development in the form of a number of guiding principles that were to govern the planning process.

Tornagrain was envisaged to be a compact town, scaled for the pedestrian rather than the motorist; it would be large enough to support an excellent range of community and leisure activities as well as economically robust enough to sustain a number of appropriate local shops. It would contain a wide, but cohesive range of homes for different household sizes and incomes and aimed

Aerial photograph of the proposed
Tornagrain site.
Courtesy The Highland Council.

to generate new employment through an integrated approach to major employment centres. Tornagrain was to have excellent public transport, walking and cycling connections to Inverness, Nairn and the Airport Business Park complex; this is part of a greater scheme of innovative environmental measures, designed to minimise consumption of natural resources and reduce dependence on mains infrastructure. This new community was also to be a centre of architectural excellence and innovation in the Highlands and Islands, complementing the surrounding landscape and taking advantage of existing buildings, views and landscape features.

From the outset, it was the Estate's aspiration that these and other attributes would encourage local town management and actively foster a sense of pride and civic responsibility in a town that would be regarded as an exemplar for a planned settlement, drawing inspiration from traditional Scottish and Highland settlements while referring to the very best contemporary practice from around the world.

Photographs taken by the project team on the various study tours:

Traditional House, Cromarty.

Winter Garden Terrace, Gassehaven, Denmark.

View towards the High Street, Dunkeld. Courtesy Moray Estates.

The initial submission to The Highland Council was issued in August 2004, and set out the argument for locating a major new settlement on land south of the Inverness Airport and its projected business park complex. In view of this, the planning policy context was outlined, and an analysis of the related transport, service infrastructure and landscape issues provided. The submission also established the proposed boundaries of the site and concluded with a set of guiding principles for development on Tornagrain as outlined above. The themes featured in this first submission were based around concepts of sustainability, efficiency of new infrastructure, the avoidance of coalescence, the identification of existing development as a nucleus for future planning and the creation of a mixed community providing homes proximate to existing, and forecasted, employment and transport opportunities.

In an effort to gain a thorough understanding of the successes and failures of planned towns, Turnberry advised the Estate to undertake a series of tours to consider other important exemplar developments. Denmark and Holland were the first countries visited, where the team saw examples of pedestrian and cyclist-oriented towns having a greater community cohesion and potential for sustainability. The team then looked comprehensively at Scotland and the rest of the UK, ultimately examining settlements from Nairn, Forres, Grantown-on-Spey, and Cromarty in the Highlands and Islands, and in Argyll and Bute, Dunkeld and Edinburgh elsewhere in Scotland, to places such as Poundbury and Hampstead Garden Suburb across the rest of the UK.

It was then that the team made a second submission to The Highland Council. This was issued in October 2004 in the form of a Case Study Report, which outlined the lessons learned through the team's tours across Europe and the United Kingdom. While no one exemplar provided a blueprint for Tornagrain, each place contained relevant and stimulating ideas, tending to reinforce the guiding principles already set out and providing a basis from which to examine prospects for success, and strategies for its achievement.

PTEa and the consultation team then began to develop an outline Masterplan for the Tornagrain site which was to include key principles to development, a density and mix of uses analysis, and a framework for open spaces and road networks. Responding positively to the site constraints and topography,

Concept Masterplan
images produced in
2004 by Pollard Thomas
Edwards architects (PTEa).
Courtesy PTEa.

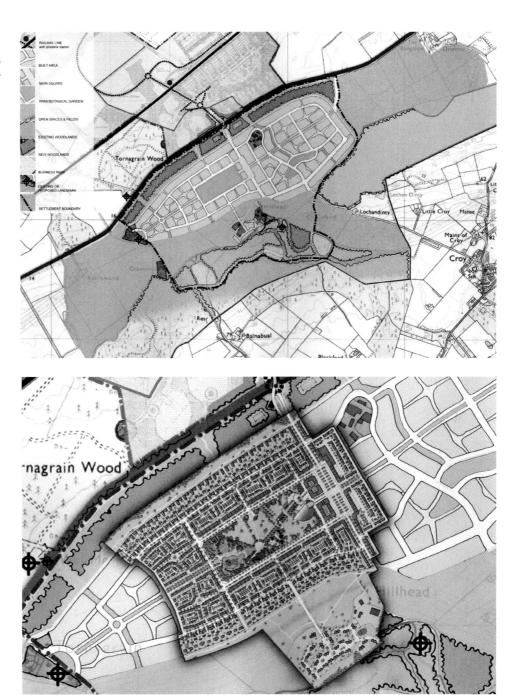

the form of the settlement began to emerge as a single, large, linear urban village comprising three main neighbourhoods and another small area adjacent to the woodland, and a fifth area on the woodland slopes to the south. The majority of the neighbourhood centres were planned to be less than ten minutes' walking distance from the principal central area of the settlement. It is estimated that one can walk 900 metres in ten minutes, so all major amenities were set to be placed within such a radius of the maximum number of town inhabitants. Additionally, the Airport Business Park is located within a five to ten minute walk from the main centre, lending a cohesion to the two developments that promises important economic advantage.

To create the critical mass to support local services (including public transport) and to sustain the urban village concept, the target population was set at 10,000 inhabitants which equates to roughly 4,650 dwellings. The strategic team undertook four density studies in relation to this objective, which clearly demonstrated that the area as defined by the proposed boundary was appropriate to create a sustainable settlement of this size, with an optimal density of approaching 30 dwellings per hectare.

Following receipt of all submissions and extensive consultation, the Council reported on the outcome of the Phase 1 study in mid-2005. This proposed a Masterplan for growth within the A96 Corridor incorporating 'polar' expansion of Inverness and Nairn, together with modest growth of established villages as well as the founding of two new settlements at Whiteness and Tornagrain.

This distribution was endorsed by The Highland Council's Director of Planning and Development in his report to committee in June 2005. This report stated that the Tornagrain site "enjoys better separation from airport activities and benefits from well-established treebelts along a significant portion of its frontage with the A96. Access into the site will be opened up by the current roadworks scheme, a sunk investment. The configuration of the land is gently undulating and rises to mature forest backdrop giving good containment and outlook."

The Council considered that the sustainable planning of these communities requires them to be closely integrated with substantial upgrading of the A96 trunk road and Aberdeen rail links together with intersecting local distributor/bus

Kentlands near Washington (top) and
Seaside in Florida (middle, bottom),
both visited as part of a comparative
tour to the United States.
Courtesy Moray Estates.

routes. It was noted that opportunities exist for new public transport interchange facilities serving these settlements. These should link residents and commuters to established (and new) sources of employment situated along the Corridor and also to higher-order commercial and public services located within the established centres of Inverness and Nairn. It was also noted that comparable enabling actions are required to build and to strengthen the key utility networks, notably electricity, water and drainage. The Highland Council formally approved the Phase 1 A96 Corridor strategy on 17 August 2005.

The Council has now moved to commissioning the Phase 2 study which is being undertaken by a team of consultants led by Halcrow.

The Phase 2 commission falls into four elements. These are the preparation of Development Framework Plans, undertaking a Strategic Environmental Appraisal of the Plans, preparation of an Implementation Programme and, lastly, the creation of a Developer Contribution Protocol. The Framework Plans will cover three issues in particular: firstly, for land generally to the east of Inverness; secondly, for the south of Nairn in the context of a new bypass around the south of the town; and thirdly, a Green Framework for the Corridor as a whole. This plan will address the proposed new communities at Whiteness and Tornagrain, as well as the business and employment allocations for the Airport and Business Park.

The implementation element will provide a coordinated programme and development phasing schedule of strategic land releases, public investment priorities and infrastructure improvements. Finally, Developer Contribution Protocol will put in place a framework governing the extent and timing of financial contributions towards public investment for each major development in the Corridor.

Prior to embarking on any response on the Phase 2 work, in autumn 2005, Turnberry with PTEa led a further comparative tour, this time to the United States. This trip took in a variety of traditionally planned towns, both old and new, including Kentlands near Washington DC, Savannah in Georgia, and Seaside, Celebration and Windsor, all in Florida. Through this trip, the Estate came into close contact with the New Urbanist Movement within the USA and in particular, with the work of Masterplanners, Duany Plater-Zyberk & Company (DPZ).

DPZ celebrated its 25th year of town planning in 2005. The company is a major leader in urban planning, having designed over 300 new and existing communities worldwide, and have received numerous highly regarded awards for their work. Needless to say, DPZ's work has therefore exerted a significant influence on the practice and direction of urban planning and development in the United States. It was clear to the Estate from the trip that this influence was starting to have a global impact, and there was much that DPZ could add to the Tornagrain project.

The firm is led by its Principals, Andres Duany and Elizabeth Plater-Zyberk, who are co-founders of the Congress for the New Urbanism (CNU), recognised by *The New York Times* as "the most important collective architectural movement in the United States in the past 50 years." New Urbanism is an international movement that seeks to end suburban sprawl and urban disinvestment. The movement, currently over 3,000 strong, marked a turning point from the segregated planning and architecture of post-war America; instead, they advocate and promote the universal and time-tested principles of planning and design that have created arguably many of the best-loved and most enduring places throughout the world.

Duany and Plater-Zyberk's recent book, *Suburban Nation*, written with Jeff Speck, was hailed in the American press as "an essential text for our time", and "a major literary event". In 2004, *Builder Magazine* recognised Duany as the fifth most influential person in home building in the USA, the ranks of which included economists, bankers and developers, as well as architects, planners and builders. Duany was the top-ranking individual from the private sector. Duany sits on the board of the National Town Builders' Association in the US, and Plater-Zyberk, as a Dean of the School of Architecture at the University of Miami, shepherds the Knight Program in Community Building, which brings an interdisciplinary approach to the revitalisation of inner cities. These and other efforts have earned Duany, Plater-Zyberk and the firm at large international recognition.

DPZ has taken a leading role in the rebuilding of the Mississippi and Louisiana coasts since Hurricanes Katrina and Rita. Working with both the Mississippi Governor's Commission on Recovery, Rebuilding and Renewal, and the Louisiana Recovery Authority, DPZ's planners and designers have generated plans for rebuilding at regional, local and neighbourhood scale. All of the work has been undertaken using the charrette methodology.

Suburban Nation, by Andres Duany,
Elizabeth Plater-Zyberk and Jeff Speck.
Courtesy and © North Point Press.

The Rise of Sprawl

SUBURBAN

and the Decline of

NATION

the American Dream

Andres Duany, Elizabeth Plater-Zyberk, and Jeff Speck

"Charrette", the French word meaning 'cart', or 'to be working against
the clock' (*etre en pleine charrette*), refers to the French School of
Beaux Arts practice wherein architecture students put their work in a
cart at deadline time. During the nineteenth century, proctors circulated
the design studios with these small carts to collect final drawings, and
students would jump on the charrette to put finishing touches on their
presentations minutes before they were due to be handed in. It was said
that the excitement of anticipation overcame the fatigue of the previous
hours of continuous work and that same level of excitement characterises
the modern charrette. The charrette is the method of planning which Duany
Plater-Zyberk & Company has adopted and developed in their traditional
planning practice. Today, designers still gather as an atelier, typically in
a single space, often on or near the project site, to study and develop
proposals in a concentrated period of time. What is new to the process is
the participation of the full communities of the projects' constituents.

The Guardian interview with
Andres Duany, published on
20 September 2006.
Courtesy Guardian Newspapers
Limited.

The Guardian | Wednesday September 20 2006

SocietyGuardian

Interview **Andres Duany**

Urban legend

The designer of Florida's much admired town Seaside, featured in The Truman Show, is now at work in
Scotland. The architect tells **Peter Hetherington** that Britain's suburban sprawl is wrong but redeemable

Portrait by David Levene

Curriculum Vitae

Age 57.

Status Married to architect Elizabeth
Plater-Zyberk.

Lives Miami.

Education Choate school, Connecticut;
Princeton University (BArch). Ecole des
Beaux Arts, Paris; Yale University
School of Architecture (MArch).

Career 1993-present: founder member,
Congress of the New Urbanism; adjunct
professor, University of Miami; 1980:
received international recognition as
designer of Seaside resort, Florida;
1980: formed architecture firm Duany
Plater-Zyberk, which built or re-
modelled 250 towns and existing communities; 1977: co-founder of architecture firm Arquitectonica with his wife
and three others.

Interests Walking around cities.

After a hectic 10 days in the Highlands planning a new town near Inverness, Andres Duany headed for London last weekend to meet the Prince of Wales. HRH wanted help with another pet project, this time affordable housing in Jamaica. Florida-based Duany, international architect, planner and co-founder of a US movement known as new urbanism, was just the man.

On first reading, his views on architecture chime neatly with those of the prince, who has embraced new urbanism. But Duany detests the ongoing battle between traditionalists and modernists – with the Prince of Wales a fierce defender of all things traditional – which has bitterly divided architecture. "What I find all over Europe, not just in Britain, is that you have architectural wars like religious wars, the theological wars of the 16th and 17th centuries. Traditionalists think modern architecture is unethical, that if you walk into a modernist building it will somehow harm you, and modernists think the reverse. Americans are more pragmatic and less ideological. We tend to combine [the two styles] and say, 'In some places a traditional building works best, in some a modernist building works best.'"

In Inverness, and in Scotland, Duany has seen the good, the bad and the plain ugly, from fine old towns and villages to awful housing – "I even visited a model house near Inverness called Miami" – that seems to replicate the worse of America. Did he, then, despair about the dismal state of new housing in Britain? "Well, no. Whatever is going wrong is very much in its early stages, whereas in America we've been going the wrong way for 45 years. Here in Britain, at least the degree of suburban sprawl that you find in places like Inverness, well, it's baby sprawl. Now it has all the elements we know will lead to the wrong kind of outcome and if you proceed in this manner long enough you will get the American condition."

Such is Duany's reputation that he has been recognised as one of the 50 most influential figures in US residential building. Born in New York and raised in Cuba, he helped found the Congress for the New Urbanism in 1993, an anti-sprawl move-

ment dedicated to reviving cities and building sustainable communities with tight design coding and good transport links to minimise car use. With his business partner and wife, fellow architect-planner Elizabeth Plater-Zyberk, he has co-designed more than 250 projects involving new towns and community regeneration schemes.

But he is best known as overall designer and planner of Seaside in Florida, a coastal new town of 4,000 immaculate, mostly holiday homes recreating a traditional southern vernacular, an early manifestation of new urbanism. Praised by an array of visiting Brits, notably the deputy prime minister, John Prescott, and Prince Charles, it was the setting for the 1990s' movie, The Truman Show, a parody of the American dream in which insurance salesman Truman Burbank (Jim Carrey) lives his life not knowing he is the star of a chilling fly-on-the-wall TV soap.

Duany has scoffed at suggestions that the planned new town near Inverness, which will include schools, shops, pubs and restaurants, will somehow replicate Seaside, which he thinks was fine for its time but, on reflection, has some flaws 25 years on. He likes to build on tradition, rather than impose some alien design on the landscape – local architects and planners will all be involved in the Highlands project – and that means not repeating the mistakes of a sprawling Inverness, the fastest growing city in Scotland.

Audacity of 'McMansion'

And for Inverness read the rest of Britain. "It has its first shopping centre, which has damaged the high street, and some very low-grade cul-de-sac residential areas. They're not even very spirited," says Duany. "One of the things you can say about America is that at least we are spirited in our commitment to suburban sprawl. Those half-apologetic sub-divisions up there [Inverness] don't even have the full vulgarity of Dallas, the audacity of the 'McMansion' [a parody of houses being churned out like burgers]. So, yeah, it's a little bit depressing to see it."

Duany's academic work, and the books he has co-authored – Suburban Nation: The Rise of Sprawl and the Decline of the American Dream – underline his commitment to new urbanism and sensitive designs, which respect local architectural

traditions. But, in part, he is a convert. In 1977, with his wife, he was co-founder of the Miami firm Arquitectonica, which became famous for what some have labelled "expressive, hi-tech modernism".

Then the couple formed Duany Plater-Zyberk and Co (DPZ) in 1980, with its headquarters in Coral Gables, Florida, changed direction dramatically, and became leaders in the new urbanist movement. But Duany does not display the zeal of the convert. Leaving Cuba in 1960 after the revolution, he eventually went to Princeton University, where he studied architecture and urban planning. After a year at the Ecole des Beaux Arts in Paris, he received a master's degree in architecture at the Yale School of Architecture.

His attitude to Cuba mirrors his pragmatism in architecture. Unlike other American-Cubans, he opposes the long-running US trade embargo on Cuba – "it just makes people angry" – and has been back to the island several times.

But he does not dwell long on his former homeland, and quickly changes tack to his passion for the legitimacy of architecture and planning. "A more interesting subject is democracy and how well, or not well, democracy works in terms of city building, particularly its inaugural moment, and there's always the problem of power – well, the centre, or the many.

"I think at the beginning, the broad layouts really do need to be centralised. Somebody needs to say, 'This shall be the centre and this shall be the edges and the main thoroughfares go this way'. [But] you can progressively download to a democratic mode if you begin being fully democratic, you know everybody gets their bit, you might not arrive at a city that works well."

Duany is well acquainted with the British system of planning. "I learned a lot from planners over here. When I went to [planning and architecture] school in the late 60s the new town movement in Britain [he mentions specifically Cumbernauld new town, near Glasgow, and Milton Keynes] was the hottest thing going in the world. So I had British professors, I had British architects at Princeton, so as it happens I am quite aware of the various British traditions, including garden cities [such as Letchworth and Welwyn in Hertfordshire].

"But working in Scotland has clearly

been an eye-opener. He admires the distinctive designs of old towns north of the border, meticulously designed to a master plan. "Scotland has an architectural tradition of consequence, a planning tradition that is still alive. Essentially it's a place that is going through a revolutionary period. It is severing its relationship to the British system, groping towards its own institutions. They're willing to change, to do things differently. England is set and Scotland, in a way, is trying to [break off] so it's an incredibly interesting time to plan in Scotland. First of all one encounters great flexibility, a willingness to do things differently."

And England? While admiring the network of green belts around cities – "we don't have them" – he thinks the overall system has disadvantages. "The way you

constrain land rather absurdly artificially raises values. Instead of going out and saying 'we need five or 7m dwellings' and laying them out efficiently so there is enough supply and the market can adjust, you have a system here that, in effect, might be the worst of both worlds."

But his affection for Britain, and Europe, remains strong. He loves its cities, culture and, most of all, its work-life balance. "Americans cannot get over how people in Europe have five weeks' vacation annually. They have no concept of quality of life, that leisure time is something to be valued. Europe is going through a spectacularly good time and its quality of life is going to be so superior to America that young people, faced with a choice of living, say, in Atlanta or Munich will choose Munich and Europe any time."

From the outset of the project, it was important to the Estate that a place was created that the Highlands could be proud of, as well as one that sat well within a hierarchy of settlements that already existed within the Corridor. Having completed the US tour and reflected on what it had seen, set against the vision and guiding principles for Tornagrain, the Estate had to determine if it wanted to involve DPZ in the next stages of development of a Masterplan for Tornagrain.

Up until this point, Moray Estates had been well served by PTEa who are highly regarded and performed very well in the early studies for the Estate. PTEa's approach was based on UK and European best practice in residential masterplanning. On completion of PTEa's work, the Estate had to determine whether the different approach of DPZ would assist the overall prospect of securing planning permission for a new town and creating a place distinct and different from UK and European best practice.

The Estate had to balance the success of DPZ in terms of experience and charrette methodology against potential criticism of involving a firm from abroad who, it could be argued, would not understand the Scottish context. After lengthy deliberation the Estate concluded that there were significant advantages of appointing DPZ and proceeded to commission them.

The research over the last three years had included trips to a multitude of places across Scotland and the UK, Europe and the US, and had included ancient towns, newly created settlements, garden cities, post-war new towns and post-war suburbia. All had proved invaluable to the Estate in their continual quest for clarity over its vision for Tornagrain. The team had looked at best practice but also examined what had not worked.

For all these trips, the focus was to understand what makes a successful town or settlement. Whilst the architecture of the places visited was important, the main focus had been on the nature, layout and urban form of places rather than individual building design. It is on these issues where judgements were made on the relative successes of particular locations as well as the lessons that could be taken forward in the town planning and charrette proposals for Tornagrain.

The research was also targeted to understand what can go wrong —
why some growing towns and cities are associated with problems such
as congestion, decline of town centres, loss of sensitive landscapes and a
poor quality built environment. It became clear to the Estate, as it has
to many others, that it is not growth in isolation that is the problem,
but the way in which growth has been accommodated. In many cases,
recent growth has created:

- Communities where it is often just too far or too difficult to walk for
  your daily needs. In short, places where you must have a car.

- Roads suffering increasing congestion because all inhabitants need
  their car to go to work, to shop or to get children to school.

- Town centres which, despite population increases, continue to
  struggle. Where retailing is moving from centres to relocate where
  car-dependent shoppers can park.

- Communities where the normal interaction of traditional towns has
  been lost as people have no access on foot to parks, shops and cafes.

- Large amounts of land consumed by development of low density
  schemes and all the infrastructure, particularly roads needed to
  serve them.

- Existing communities can continue to grow like this and some
  economic advantages may occur because of it, but congestion will
  increase, town centres will struggle to survive, despite the best efforts
  of many, and people will become ever more reliant on their cars.

The team believed that with the creation of a planned new town at Tornagrain,
growth could be accommodated in a form that would overcome the
problems set out above, and instead create an attractive place to live. This
desire for change in the way towns are planned aligned itself closely to the
principles of New Urbanism and the work of Andres Duany and DPZ.

At Tornagrain, the Estate is firmly committed to a pattern of growth that will:

- Optimise its excellent transport links, particularly rail, to allow people to travel to Inverness centre, to work or shop, without using their car.

- Be compact and walkable, with streets and roads designed to accommodate the car, not for the car.

- Provide for people's daily needs within a comfortable walking distance.

- Have jobs in close proximity to where people live, at the Business Park and within the community.

- Reduce land used for development through compactness and dense development.

Sketch drawings of possible house types, produced during the Charrette held in September 2006. Courtesy Duany Plater-Zyberk & Company (DPZ).

Ultimately, the DPZ appointment was made by the Estate in February 2006. At that time, it was also agreed that the charrette process should be held during a nine day period at the beginning of September 2006.

The August 2006 paper distributed to the local community promoting the Charrette. Courtesy Moray Estates.

In preparation for this event, the Estate made a series of specialist consultant appointments to ensure a full understanding of the site including all physical and technical constraints and opportunities would be available to the team in time for the Charrette. This research included:

- An analysis of the population forecasts for the A96 Corridor including population modelling. This work clarified the Council's forecast of 30,000 growth in 30–40 years as broadly robust.

- A detailed examination of important elements of the landscape, archaeology, local heritage and biodiversity on the site including habitat mapping. All of these studies provided a clear picture of the physical constraints and opportunities relevant to the site and surrounding area.

- The principles of transport and surface access strategy, which was adopted through analysis and consultation with key groups including the Council, Scottish Executive and local public transport companies and groups.

- A socio-economic impact assessment to identify the social, economic and community based demands that need to be satisfactorily addresses to maximise the potential for the site. A key part of this was the requirement to examine the local economic base to examine strengths and weaknesses.

- A consolation of the research into the architecture, design and urban form of the built environment in the Highlands, as well as New Urbanist Towns in Europe and the USA, that have been visited by both the Estate and Turnberry.

In June 2006, and with the lead up to the Charrette well underway, Turnberry and Moray Estates coordinated a fact finding and project familiarisation tour for the DPZ team. In addition to a detailed review of the site, surrounding area and A96 Corridor region in general, the tour included further visits to a number of planned settlements that had already formed part of the Estate's research effort. These included Dunkeld, Cromarty, Nairn, Forres and Edinburgh, all in Scotland. The trip also incorporated a series of lectures given by Andres Duany on the principles of New Urbanism in Inverness, Edinburgh and London. The lecture in Inverness was a public event at the UHI Millennium Institute and had the greatest attendance of any of the public programmes.

In August, a paper was issued promoting the Charrette. This was posted to around 7,000 homes in the A96 corridor. It was produced by both Turnberry and the Estate and provided essential background information on the Estate's aspirations for Tornagrain, the research undertaken, the current status of the Council's planning for growth within the corridor, as well as a detailed programme of activity for the Charrette itself.

The Charrette itself was officially opened by Jim MacKinnon, the Chief Planner at the Scottish Executive. It began with an opening presentation which was delivered by Andres Duany on the evening of 5 September, to an audience of approaching 200. The presentation sought to explain how the Charrette would work as well as providing a brief introduction to the principles of good urban planning. It also explained in detail how the programme for the Charrette was to work.

Sketch drawings of possible house types, produced during the Charrette held in September 2006.
Courtesy DPZ.

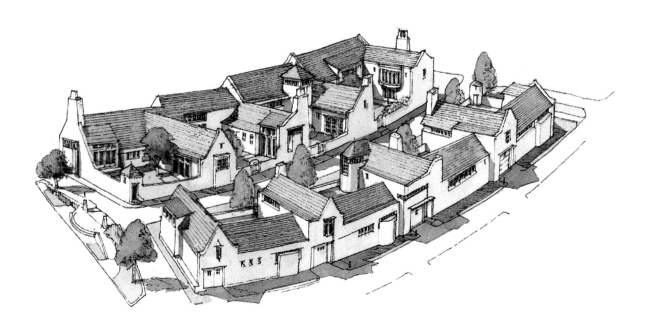

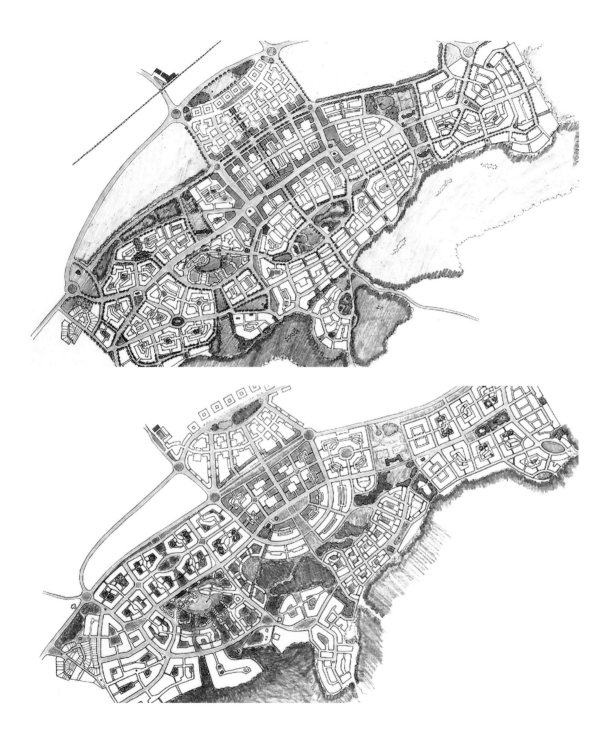

Opposite: Two emerging Masterplan options presented at the mid-term 'pin-up' during the Charrette of September 2006. Courtesy DPZ.

The design team then started work immediately producing masterplan options and design. The options were informed by formal and informal meetings with local consultees ranging from the local authority, community groups, government agencies and businesses. The design team's proposals and strategies were "reality tested" on a daily basis to prevent unacceptable schemes progressing too far. The unusual aspect of the consultation process was the ability of the public to interact with the design team and raise relevant issues at any point without limitation. This continued throughout the Charrette.

A mid term 'pin-up' took place on Sunday 9 September. This was a crucial part of the Charrette, where the designers were given the opportunity to display their approach to development so far. This provided the public and related parties and participants of the Charrette, the possibility to respond immediately to the designs — and gain feedback on their response.

Architectural rendering of a possible urban design solution produced during the Charrette of September 2006. Courtesy DPZ.

A final presentation was then given on the last night of the Charrette, when nearly all of the work produced during the Charrette was presented and explained.

The Masterplan put forward at the
closing presentation of the Charrette.
Courtesy DPZ.

A series of sketches showing possible house types such as a crescent and a terrace, and exploring local materials, such as wood and corrugated metal for roofs, produced during the Charrette of September 2006.
Courtesy DPZ.

The conclusion of the Charrette was met with a mixture of relief and delight. There is no doubt that from the Estate's perspective, it had been a success. This can be measured on many levels. The process had captured the attention of the public and all of the presentations and public meetings had been well attended. There had also been a high level of engagement and debate. At times, there had been concern or disagreement voiced by some within the communities local to the site, but most who participated agreed on one issue — the process had been open and had given people an opportunity to have their say.

The proposals for Tornagrain and the Charrette had also captured the attention of the media, with coverage on Channel 4 News, as well as both national and local press and radio.

Now that the Charrette has finished, DPZ has a remit to review the images produced and refine the masterplan to a finished document ready for production by the end of 2006. This will then form the key element of the submission made to The Highland Council as part of the Phase 2 process.

There is clearly still a long way to go before the Estate can start to plan the delivery of Tornagrain with any certainty. However, with the help and support of its principal advisors, Turnberry, it remains as committed as ever to its vision for a new town in the Highlands.

Proposed new teaching and screening building for the National Film and Television School at Beaconsfield. Courtesy Glenn Howells Architects.

National Film and Television School

Since its formation in 1971 the National Film and Television School (NFTS) has become the UK's centre for excellence in media education and training. Students are able to practise television and filmmaking in industry-standard facilities, where working methods model professional practice. Alumni of the School have gone on to produce successful British and Hollywood films and TV productions as well as pop promos, commercials and video games. The School's bridges to industry bring film companies and broadcasters together with new talent through initiatives like development deals, short script competitions, opportunities with Channel 4 and MTV and mentoring relationships with major industry players.

NFTS is fortunate in that the Beaconsfield site was previously a fully functional film studio, starting from the time that George Clark Productions established the site as Beaconsfield Studios in 1921. The British Lion Film Corporation then took occupancy of the site in 1929, under the Chairmanship of prolific thriller writer Edgar Wallace. During the Second World War the site was requisitioned by the Ministry of Works to make aircraft magnetos for the war effort, but soon after the end of the War, the Crown Film Unit occupied the site with significant Government spending allocated for its refurbishment. In 1951, the organisation disbanded but, meanwhile, the National Film Finance Corporation formed Group 3 with a brief to encourage new British talent. Their occupancy proved to be a short one, lasting only two years from 1953 to 1955, when it was decided that a studio base was unjustifiable for the organisation's activities. Television first found Beaconsfield Studios in 1957 when Screen Gems rented the space to make their *Ivanhoe* TV series starring Roger Moore. The final production company to reside at Beaconsfield Studios was Independent Artistes who hosted a respectable run of films, ending with *Press for Time*, 1966, the final film shot on the site. In 1961, North Thames Gas Board leased the premises as a warehouse until the NFTS took occupancy in 1971, founding its unique educational practice.

NFTS is unusual among film schools in providing purpose-built film studios, separate large TV studios and other facilities to best train in new media's various areas of specialisation. The studios are fitted with computerised lighting rigs, lightweight cameras and a gallery that houses sound, vision and lighting equipment. The Production Design Department boasts a fully-equipped, interactive design studio with 2-D and 3-D computer graphic systems, while the Animation Department is served by a 35 mm rostrum camera and three

Aerial view of the National Film and
Television School at Beaconsfield.
Courtesy and © Simmons Aerofilms.

The White House building at the Ealing Film Studios, which historically was the head office for the Studios, where Sir Michael Balcon produced many of the famous Ealing comedies. Courtesy National Film and Television School.

35 mm stop-motion animation cameras, along with various image manipulation and origination software necessary for a complete education in the field. Screenwriters and production students benefit from several Movie Magic suites, equipped with the latest industry software, while budding cinematographers have a range of film and digital cameras at their disposal, and a wide array of grip and lighting equipment. A sophisticated stock of track-laying systems is made available to students of Sound Production, complemented by a Dolby Surround Sound dubbing theatre and a second, smaller, sound theatre. Composers studying at the school work in cabins equipped with electronic keyboards and computerised sampling systems while having access to an exclusive orchestral library with six adjacent music

studios. The students can view the fruits of their labour in an industry-standard screening theatre which projects films, tape, laser disc and DVD, or in a number of seminar rooms complete with screen monitors and playback facilities.

Although the NFTS has much to be proud of, in the 1990s it became apparent that some of the facilities had become substandard, which deviated from the School's unique reputation of facility excellence and detracted from its ability to attract a high level of student and staff in an increasingly competitive higher-learning and international marketplace. The School's present reception is in the middle of the site and attempts to control access to the space through a camera link with the main entrance, a strategy that has led to several recent thefts of professional equipment and is therefore considered inadequate. Further, the current screening theatre is incapable of surround sound (which has become the industry standard) and the layout of the library generates poor access for students and staff. In terms of ancillary buildings, the canteen dates back to 1941 and has a rotting and sodden sleeper foundation, along with an inefficient configuration, and there are presently no common rooms for the use of staff and students.

In the early 1990s, the School acquired Ealing Film Studios and ran it as an operational studio whilst it prepared its plans for a new School on the site. The plans for a relocation to Ealing were predicated by a substantial lottery grant for equipment and feasibility. Ultimately the School could not demonstrate a feasible scheme for Ealing and, once this was clear, Turnberry advised the School on the sale of the Ealing site.

For these and other reasons the NFTS decided in the early 1990s that a strategy for change needed to be put in place to ensure the provision of facilities that befitted the status of the School and its international reputation. Through that time, Turnberry has worked with the School to identify a development solution best fitting its needs. To fund the proposed London relocation the NFTS sought to enhance through the town planning process the value of the Beaconsfield site. To achieve this, Turnberry participated in the South Bucks District Council Local Plan process, and as such, achieved a residential allocation for the Beaconsfield site. After Ealing, the School had two further schemes to move to London, one as part of the Rick Mather South Bank Masterplan, and the second to St George's Circus on land owned by South Bank University. All proved difficult due to the funding gap between the available assets and the cost of a new building.

Wallace and Gromit, created by
Nick Park, an NFTS alumni.
Courtesy and © Aardman Animations.

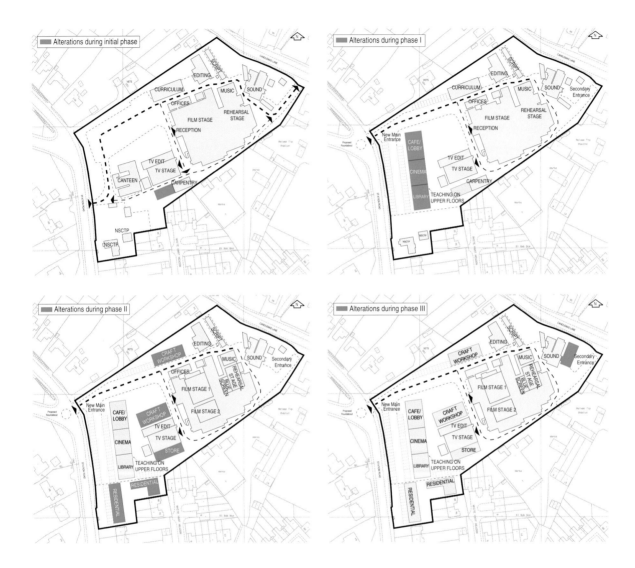

Outline Masterplan showing the initial
proposals for the phased redevelopment
of Beaconsfield Studios.
Courtesy David Edmonds.

Eventually it was decided that the School would be better served, at least in the short and medium term, if it were to remain at Beaconsfield and embark on a cost-effective programme to refurbish its current facilities.

Following its decision to remain, the NFTS produced a masterplan to guide the phased redevelopment of its facilities and buildings at the Beaconsfield site. Phase 1 proposes the construction of a new education building toward the front of the site, accommodating new teaching facilities, support functions and a cinema equipped to seat around 150 people. The completion of this new building will facilitate the relocation of all site administration, office and classroom teaching facilities from other parts of the site while providing flexibility to improve the vacated spaces within the craft and production buildings. Phase 2 involves the creation of a new craft building and a new lighting and scenery store while a concurrent refurbishment of the existing film stage building will be undertaken. Phase 3 sees improvements made to the post-production buildings at the eastern boundary of the site, which is likely to include extensions to the existing sound buildings although the precise requirements of these additions have yet to be determined.

For the first phase, Turnberry worked with the School to put in place a project team led by architects Glenn Howells. The aims and objectives of the client were then brought into focus, emerging as a desire to restructure the site's layout into the three distinct functions of teaching, production and public access in one new three-storey building, and to wherever possible refurbish and enhance the efficiency of the existing buildings. It is also the School's aim to provide for enhanced production facilities that will enable more formal craft training, and to use the existing production facilities for short courses and workshop production assistant learning. Further, the creation of a modest screening and conference facility is envisioned, which will enable the site to facilitate greater community access in view of enhancing the School's role as a national site for film and television training and research. To complement these improvements, the NFTS will also remove two temporary buildings (the canteen and the catering block) and replace them with a cafe and restaurant facility within the proposed new building giving rise to better planning for the site as a whole.

Plan of the Beaconsfield site, illustrating
the Phase 1 proposals — the new teaching
and screening building. The existing short
course teaching site, which was sold in
Summer 2006, is outlined in red.
Courtesy Glenn Howells Architects.

Architectural visualisation of the cafe and dining area in the new teaching and screening building. Courtesy Glenn Howells Architects.

There were several policy considerations that needed to be addressed in the planning for the NFTS redevelopment. Firstly, whilst the application proposes an increase in the total floor space at the School's site, the new building does not represent an expansion of the School or a change in its aims of use. Rather the redevelopment is an attempt to provide the necessary improvements to the facilities needed to support the School's current operations. The Local Plan provides general guidance on design considerations relevant to any new buildings, which is consistent with the School's plans to provide a new construction of higher architectural standard within the height and mass parameters of buildings currently on the site. Building form and design was also a matter of policy consideration, with the Local Plan indicating that the new development should be of an aesthetic nature that harmonises with the surrounding properties, including any buildings retained on the site. While the redevelopment at the NFTS represents a step-change in the quality of architecture on the Beaconsfield site, the School intends to use modern materials in keeping with the surrounding buildings and in so doing hopes to enhance the aesthetic quality of the area in general. In terms of access and parking issues, the School's proposal represents

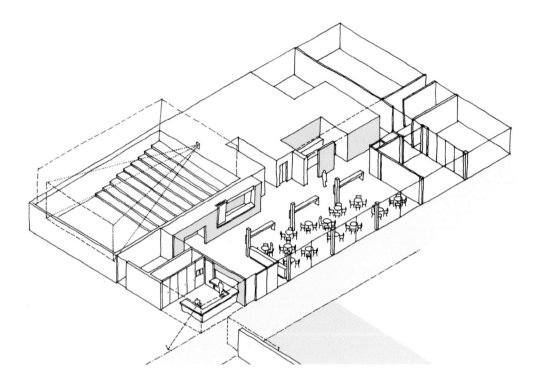

Architectural visualisation of the
ground floor of the new teaching
and screening building.
Courtesy Glenn Howells Architects.

a significant improvement to the safety, convenience and aesthetic quality of
the footways and footpaths across the site and, while there is a planned minor
reduction in the available parking spaces, the NFTS has an excellent track record
of public transport use and does not use its existing parking facilities to their
current capacity. Relevant to the School's security issues, the redevelopment also
seeks to provide a more secure site without unduly restricting access to the area,
and without the introduction of unsightly and draconian security measures.

In addition to the town planning considerations, Turnberry has also worked
closely with the School in putting together a funding package and ensuring
that the Phase 1 development is deliverable. As part of this process, Turnberry
has advised on the sale of part of the existing Beaconsfield site to generate
funds and has also sat on the Steering Board which has had the specific
remit of ensuring the Phase 1 building is delivered on programme and
budget. The new building is scheduled for completion in Autumn 2007.

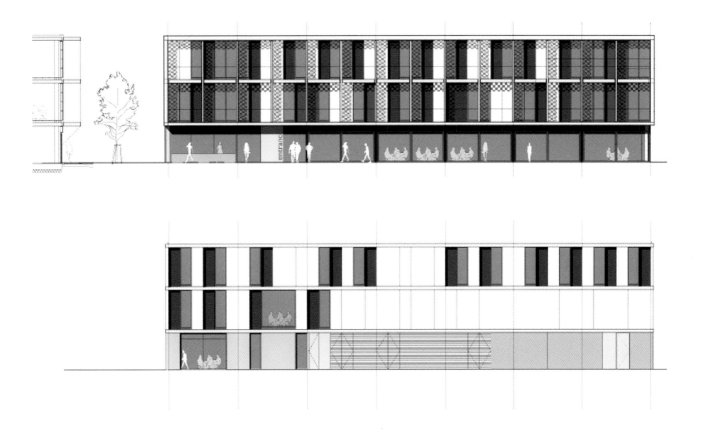

Proposed elevations of the new teaching and screening building. Courtesy Glenn Howells Architects.

The Masterplan redevelopment taken as a whole will include improved security and reception areas, a foyer and exhibition hall, a cafe facility, a new library, improved cinema and projection rooms, an improved Short Course Unit, new seminar and meeting rooms, improved viewing rooms, curriculum offices, tutor rooms and new student bases. The positioning of the new building will contribute towards a more coherent layout of the site, allowing both better legibility and accessibility through the site along with increased security provisions. This will provide the NFTS with the facilities and support it requires to maintain its reputation of excellence and enable it to compete successfully as the national leader in film and television education for the twenty-first century.

Aerial photograph of Inverness Airport. Courtesy John Paul Photography

Inverness Airport
Business Park and
Inverness Airport

Inverness Airport Business Park

The Inverness Airport Business Park (IABP) is a joint venture company comprising Highlands and Islands Airports Limited (HIAL), Highlands and Islands Enterprise Inverness and East Highland (HIE-IEH), and Moray Estates. The company was formed to progress the development of the 250-hectare site adjacent to Inverness Airport, located seven miles to the northeast of Inverness and immediately north of the A96.

In July 2001, Turnberry Consulting was appointed to undertake a feasibility study for a project that was little more than an outline vision and an area of search identified in the Draft Inverness Local Plan. The feasibility study amounted to an investigation into the viability of progressing a project like IABP, including advice on the corporate and developmental infrastructure required to push the scheme forward. In order to come to relevant conclusions the feasibility study involved several dimensions of enquiry, beginning with separate discussions with each partner in order to establish their individual objectives for the project.

Once Turnberry had an idea of the particular concerns and aims of each party it then set up a group meeting to agree upon a joint statement of objectives for the scheme and an effective mechanism for its advancement. In a separate exercise to assess the project's viability, Turnberry studied various reports looking at the demand for employment in the Inverness area, the availability of corporate accommodation and the growth prospects for Inverness in particular and the region as a whole. Ultimately, Turnberry presented a plan for implementation for the IABP scheme which included comment on the procurement of a new access road to broaden the area's development potential (while providing better access to the airport), the long process of obtaining permissions from the relevant planning authorities, and advice on unifying all of the interested parties in a sustainable and efficient structure.

Through this initial analysis, it was clear that the priority for the project was the construction of a new road, which involved the collaboration of all parties (including The Highland Council) to provide the necessary financial support and land use, with a concurrent funding appeal to the European Regional Development Fund (ERDF). The key element to achieving a consensus over a short period was an innovative approach by which Turnberry and Burness, the Group solicitors, acted jointly for all parties whilst they retained their original advisors. There is a history in

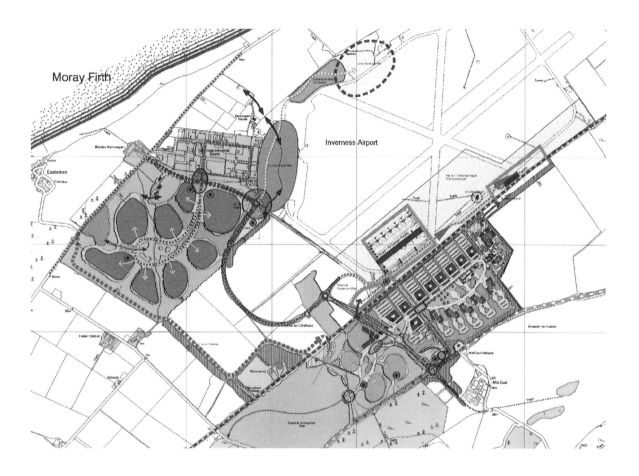

Concept Masterplan for the Inverness Airport
Business Park (IABP) produced to support
the outline planning application.
Courtesy and © Barton Wilmore Partnership.

the UK of multi-party joint venture discussions stalling over many years. The new
approach was to try and break the problem of a failure to agree. The subsequent
negotiations were difficult and protracted, but ultimately successful, albeit with
changes from the original principles with The Highland Council providing loan
stock to the joint venture company to facilitate the construction of the road. The
road was completed in Spring 2005. Throughout this period, Turnberry advised
on the entire process leading to the creation of the joint venture company. In order
to accomplish this goal, Turnberry advised on the appointment and management
of a solicitor to the consortium, led the negotiations toward an agreement on the
Heads of Terms, and worked with the legal team in the subsequent production of
all other necessary legal agreements.

In a separate undertaking, Turnberry appointed a planner to co-ordinate and progress an outline planning application for the park as whole, as well as assist in the creation of a masterplan which proposes a 30 year development programme for uses that include light industrial units, hotel and conferencing facilities, a rail station, air freight facilities, aircraft maintenance operations, and a business and research park. Whilst the planning permission has still to be obtained, the site is now allocated for IABP in the adopted Inverness Local Plan, and the development has been factored into the overall vision for growth within the A96 Corridor and Inner Moray Firth area. The company is now operational with its own members of staff and has retained Turnberry to provide strategic advice on the first phases of development.

When completed, it is likely that around 260,000 square metres of accommodation will have been developed, supporting up to 5,000 full-time jobs.

The site may become more integrated in the planned new town at Tornagrain, maximising the prospect of success. IABP is now in the process of masterplanning the site, disposing of some of the early schemes and identifying a development partner.

Aerial view showing the new access road.
Courtesy and © John Paul Photography.

Inverness Airport

Inverness Airport is located immediately to the north of IABP and Tornagrain. Highlands and Islands Airports Limited (HIAL) is a Scottish Executive-owned company charged with the operation and development of a network of ten airports across the Highlands and Islands of Scotland. Inverness is the biggest of these airports, where annual passenger levels are expected to approach the 800,000 mark for the year ending March 2007. This represents a growth of the order of 85 per cent over the past five years, making it the fastest growing airport in Scotland in both 2004 and 2005. Against this background, in late 2004 HIAL appointed Turnberry to work on the preparation of a Masterplan to guide the expansion of the airport over a 25 year period up to 2030.

The requirement for a Masterplan had been principally driven by the White Paper on Air Transport, published by the Government in December 2003, which set a requirement for all airports of a certain size to produce a Masterplan within a certain timeframe. A subsequent guidance document was issued by the Department of Transport in 2004, which set out more specific parameters for the production and delivery of airport masterplans. This second document specifically identified the Airport at Inverness as a location obligated to produce a Masterplan of this nature. With a clear mandate, Turnberry and HIAL set out to deliver a cohesive and effective Masterplan that would provide for the smooth evolution of Inverness Airport over the next 25 years. The Masterplan process essentially fell into two stages, the first involving an extensive internal discussion and debate within HIAL to align aims and produce an outline Masterplan. Thereafter the Masterplan progressed through the consultation of key stakeholders, an analysis of the impact the development proposals might have on the region, as well as any mitigation strategy that would need to be implemented to address these issues as they arose. Ultimately, Turnberry advanced a consultation programme leading up to HIAL's adoption of the Masterplan as a confirmed policy for Inverness Airport.

In order to get a sense of the character and standard of similarly-sized airports in the UK, Turnberry led a case study tour with executive members from HIAL visiting airports at Exeter, Cork and Bristol. This exercise yielded valuable information on the pitfalls and successes of planning for growth

View of Inverness Airport terminal.
Courtesy Highlands and Islands Airports Ltd.

at airports of a similar scale to the proposed development at Inverness. HIAL, in conjunction with Turnberry, appointed architects Bennetts Associates to work on the first phase exercise and produce a series of plans illustrating the growth of the Airport to 2030. The study grew out of an investigation into the various activities, uses and component parts of the Airport, in an effort to gain an understanding of how growth would occur over the three phases of development, to 2010, 2020 and 2030. This study culminated in a report that featured a matrix of proposals for change over the defined phases, as well as an implementation plan for advancing the scheme at key junctions in its development. This report was then ratified by the HIAL Board and Turnberry were retained to advise on the second phase which involved the preparation of a more detailed Masterplan that would satisfy the criteria set out by the Department for Transport.

This process has been continuous through 2005 and 2006, involving various dimensions of project management and planning consultation. Turnberry acted for HIAL in the appointment of a series of specialist consultants to investigate different dimensions of the proposal, including landscape and ecology concerns, surface access and transportation, socio-economic impact, air quality and noise issues. Turnberry, in conjunction with the various specialists they appointed,

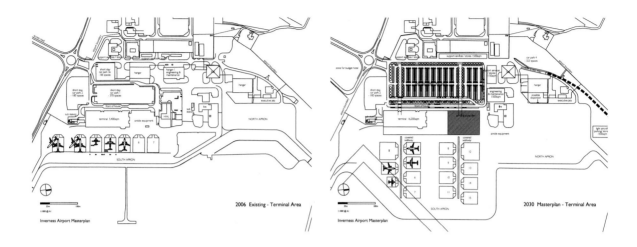

Inverness Airport as currently laid out in 2006 and in 2030 after completion of the third phase of development. Courtesy Bennetts Associates.

produced reports on each of these dimensions, along with associated mitigation strategies that might be required as the scheme progressed and the airport grew to its forecasted size. In the meantime Turnberry and HIAL were also conducting in-depth consultations with all of the key stakeholders in the Inverness Airport scheme, including the Scottish Executive, the Highland Council, HIE-IEH and HIE, HITRANS (strategic transport partnership). The results of these consultations were used to inform the shape of the maturing Masterplan, and to anticipate potential problems therein. Similarly, Turnberry undertook consultation with key airport operators including all of the major airlines like BA Connect, easyJet, bmi, Eastern Airways, Loganair, and Highland Airways. This investigation proved essential in gaining an understanding of Inverness Airport's potential corporate affiliates, the commercial objectives and industry expectations of a future airport development.

HIAL, in conjunction with Turnberry finalised a report for the purposes of public consultation in autumn 2006. An exhibition of proposals was then held in the main terminal building. The public consultation exercise was designed to provide a forum for local and regional concern regarding the proposed development, while at the same time providing a mechanism to build solutions to such complications before they arise. The Masterplan will be adopted by HIAL and submitted to the Department for Transport by the end of 2006.

View of the Octagon taken from the beam
floor in the Beam Engine House at Crossness.
Courtesy Crossness Engines Trust.

Crossness Engines Trust

The summer of 1858 was particularly hot. At this time the River Thames was a vast open sewer with all the contents of London's WCs and cesspits emptying into local drains which in turn discharged directly into the river. As a result, foul smells always lingered over the city and illnesses like cholera and typhoid claimed many lives through several epidemics. Matters came to a head when a stench from the River Thames passing the Houses of Parliament became unbearable and in an attempt to alleviate the resulting discomfort, the windows were draped with curtains soaked in deodorising chemicals, but still MPs were at times forced to leave the chamber entirely.

The Government called upon the chief of the Metropolitan Board of Works, Sir Joseph Bazalgette, to find a solution to London's sewage problem and to rid the city of its unpleasant odours and filthy streets. A brand new sewerage system was designed which encompassed a network of new drains running into a vast sewer made of engineering bricks, and using newly developed Portland cement as mortar. Sewage ran through these large tunnels and, with the aid of gravity, along both sides of the Thames, travelling eastward to Crossness on the south

Reservoir under construction, c.1864.
Courtesy Crossness Engines Trust.

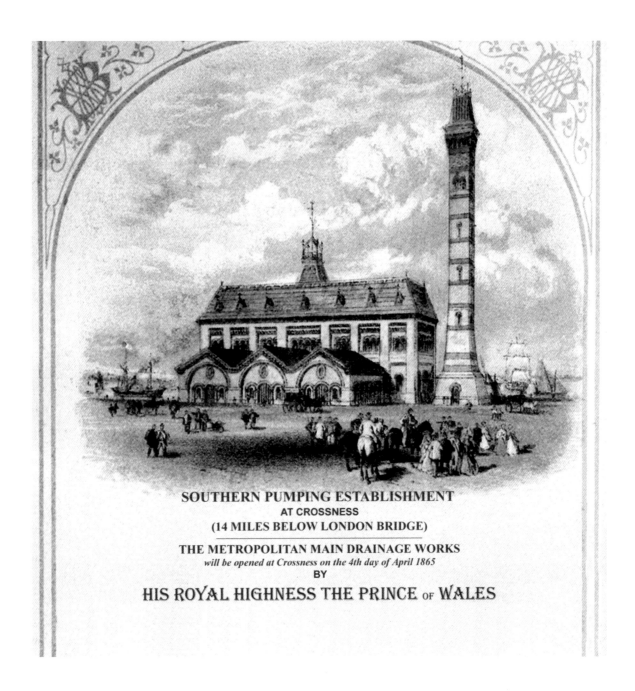

Poster promoting the opening of Crossness in 1865.
Courtesy Crossness Engines Trust.

Artist's impression of Crossness in
the early twentieth century.
Courtesy Crossness Engines Trust.

bank, and to Barking on the north. At Crossness, the sewage was pumped into
a covered reservoir and held until an ebb tide when it was released into the
Thames to be taken away toward the North Sea. Four huge pumping engines
(each named after a member of the Royal Family) were constructed for this
task, and a flamboyant Victorian building was designed to house them. The
benefits to London's inhabitants was enormous; not only did the quality of
drinking water improve, and the streets become cleaner and more pleasant,
but also (and perhaps most importantly) there was only one more serious
outbreak of cholera after Bazalgette's pumping stations were operational.

The original 1864 buildings at Crossness formed an elegant group, standing
a few yards from the River Thames on Erith Marshes. Many of these buildings
still stand today. The Engine House itself was some 46 metres in length built
on two floors, together with a boiler room to house the 12 Cornish boilers

required to raise the necessary steam power. Immediately to the south of the Boiler House is a terraced garden, at either end of which stand single storey Grade II listed buildings constructed in a style sympathetic to that of the Engine House. There are three external entrances to the Engine House; one at each end of the building, and the main door, which faces the river and is now obscured by the Triple Expansion Engine House built in 1898, masking the entrance's grand design. At the west end of the garden is the Valve House, which had several different functions over the years, first to house some of the control machinery for the penstocks, then as an engine house, later as a garage and finally as a marine store. The Fitting Shop is found to the east end of the garden and has remained relatively unaltered since its construction; the addition of some lime stores beneath the floor is virtually invisible, though a smithy added to the north side in 1912 is quite apparent.

South of the Valve House's terraced garden and Fitting Shop is the subterranean reservoir, which at 170 by 165 metres has a capacity of 25 million gallons. The reservoir is covered in soil and turf, and houses built for the workers were built at the top of its western boundary. There were also some grander houses built on the reservoir for the Gasman and the Works Superintendent. The interior of the Engine House itself is a striking example of Victorian design, with decorative friezes, columns and cast-iron screens, giving rise to the building's moniker 'The Crossness Cathedral'.

Left: The beam floor with Alexandra's beam in the foreground and Albert Edward's beam in the background. Courtesy Crossness Engines Trust.

Right: Prince Consort's main beam. Courtesy Crossness Engines Trust.

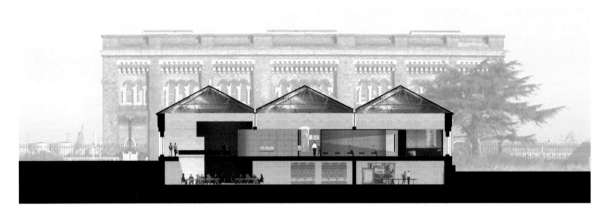

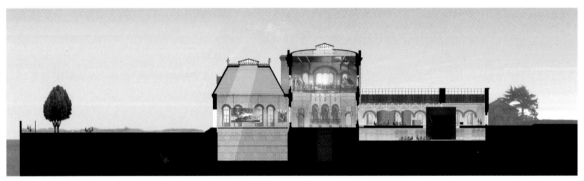

Benson + Forsyth's illustration of the changes proposed to the Crossness buildings which are the subject of the Heritage Lottery Fund bid. Courtesy Benson + Forsyth.

Today the Crossness Engines are certainly the largest surviving rotative beams in the world, and the only remaining original set, therefore preservation of this unique piece of heritage has become of paramount importance. From 1956, when the engines ceased to be used, until 1985, the Engine House was abandoned and its contents left vulnerable to vandalism and decay.

The Crossness Engines Trust was established in 1987 with the primary aim of conserving the Crossness Pumping Station site, and shortly after its formation a lengthy restoration of one of the engines (the "Prince Consort") was undertaken. At the same time a proportion of the decorative ironwork in the Engine House was stripped of rust and repainted in colours approximating those originally used. However, years of disuse and disrepair have taken their toll, and the buildings themselves are now considered "at risk" by English Heritage.

View of the Crossness site, 2006.
Courtesy Benson + Forsyth.

It is the vision and the aim of the Crossness Engines Trust to realise the potential of the site, recreating the space as a place where people learn and are inspired while appreciating the historical foundations of one of London's most impressive engineering constructions. The overarching objective is to restore and maintain the buildings, engines, site and collections at Crossness and to ultimately achieve Registered Museum Status.

Today, the Trust is chaired by Peter Bazalgette, great great grandson of Sir Joseph. Bazalgette is also a Governor to the National Film and Television School, and it is through this connection that Turnberry was invited to work with the team in developing the plans for restoration.

With the help of Turnberry Consulting, in 2005 the Trust prepared a submission of a Stage 1 funding application to the Heritage Lottery Fund (HLF) for assistance with their first phase of construction: conservation of the core buildings; enhancement of the visitor experience; improved access; landscaping; and the recruitment of a professional team to undertake the necessary operations. To support their application, the Trust appointed architects Benson + Forsyth to design the new visitor centre and exhibition space, as well as oversee the much-needed conservation works. With the team in place, spearheaded by experienced Tourism and Heritage Consultant Michael Nutt, the Trust won their bid to the HLF in June 2005.

The Trust's plans have implications across the Thames Gateway. Indeed related proposals to develop a community arts facility on the site will provide another means to make Crossness more attractive to new visitors. The improved exhibition and refurbished site will encourage better understanding of the site's heritage, while extended opening hours, improved access, better marketing and an upgraded website will further widen the opportunity for visitors to appreciate the site's heritage. Considerable investment is also planned for the regeneration and transport infrastructure of this part of London.

The Trust sees Crossness as enhancing the area's emerging visitor economy, as well as contributing significantly to the local and regional community, including social benefits in the form of educational and training initiatives, and environmental benefits in terms of contributing to the enhancement of the Thames Path route. The Trust is currently working with its design and project team on the next level of detailed analysis. To this end, it has set up a steering group made of Trustees and specialist advisors to help guide the team towards the submission of the Stage 2 Heritage Lottery Fund application for funding. If approved, the Trust hopes to move towards the implementation of the first phase of its vision for Crossness at some point during 2007 and it will contribute significantly to the funding package to enable this very important project to proceed.

The Octagon in the Beam Engine House at Crossness.
Courtesy Crossness Engines Trust.

Epilogue

This book has focused on only a small number of Turnberry projects. There are many other clients and projects that have contributed to the success of the company since its inception in 1998. Brief mention of a number of these is included below.

In 2006, Turnberry began advising **Arlington** on the preparation of a fund dedicated to investment in the development of Science and Technology Parks across the UK. For the **British Airports Authority**, Turnberry advised on a strategy for the expansion of the Turnhouse cargo area at Edinburgh Airport. Turnberry has assisted the **British Olympic Association** on the establishment of a Centre of Excellence for minority sports training at Upper Heyford in Oxfordshire, and **Castleford Tigers Rugby Football League Club**, on a scheme for the development of a new stadium for the Club.

Turnberry has advised **Cranfield University** on property and development issues since 1998, including the creation and development of the Technology Park, consolidation of campus sites in Bedfordshire, operational planning issues associated with the academic estate, and planning and disposal advice on surplus land assets.

In early 2006, Turnberry obtained planning permission for the proposed **Castle Stuart Golf Links** in the Highlands, a development comprising two championship courses, hotel and spa, and fractional ownership properties.

Turnberry obtained planning permission for a new Foster and Partners-designed 2,000 pupil Academy at Peterborough for the **Department for Education and Skills**, following which advice was provided to the DfES on a similar scheme in Corby, Northamptonshire.

Turnberry has acted for **GSK plc** in respect of its manufacturing facility in Dartford, Kent since 1998. In addition to a variety of operational planning and property issues, this work has recently involved the sale of surplus land including the nearby sports and social club. The current focus is on a planning strategy for the disposal of a now redundant part of the factory site extending to over 15 hectares and adjacent to Dartford town centre.

In addition to the Centre for Health Sciences, Turnberry is currently advising **HIE-Inverness and East Highlands** on a Masterplan for the development of new facilities for Inverness College and the University of Highlands and Islands, together with a research park.

Turnberry advised the **International Cricket Council** on the preparation of Minimum Standards to manage the issue of players' and officials' safety at Test and One Day International grounds. It was also the planning advisor responsible for obtaining planning permission on behalf of **Ipswich Town Football Club** for the redevelopment of part of the Portman Road Stadium.

In 2004, Turnberry was commissioned by the charity, **John Grooms**, on the development of a new care home in Southend. Since 2000, it has advised **Mid Suffolk District Council** on a variety of strategic development issues across the district including a development agreement to facilitate the regeneration of an important part of historic Stowmarket town centre.

Another early commission was for **NM Rothschild** on the development and financing of a major office waterfront scheme in Guernsey.

In 2005, Turnberry worked with the **Northern Racing College** to produce a Masterplan for the development of an enhanced training facility, visitor centre and country park, for its estate south of Doncaster.

For **Perkins Engines**, part of the Caterpillar group of companies, Turnberry is preparing a strategic property review for the principal manufacturing estate in Peterborough. And Turnberry is also currently advising the **Oxford School of Islamic Studies** on a strategy for development of surplus land in central Oxford.

In 2000, Turnberry acted for the **Rugby Football League**, **Rugby Football Union** and the **University of Manchester** on the creation of a new Centre of Excellence for both rugby codes as part of the UK Sports Institute.

For **Scottish Enterprise — Edinburgh & Lothian**, Turnberry undertook an original research exercise into the linkage between universities and medi-parks, and in addition, acted for **Scottish Enterprise Grampian** on the preparation of a Development Strategy for the future of the two Science Parks in Aberdeen.

Turnberry is currently appointed as a Panel Advisor to **Sport England** for planning appeals in the south east of England. The advice also included assistance with the planning and associated development that will govern the potential for selected National Centres at Lilleshall and Holmepierrepoint.

Whilst Turnberry's involvement with the **University of Oxford** has already been detailed in respect of certain projects, it is important to mention a variety of other schemes including planning permission for a new Biochemistry facility and planning advice for a new building for Earth Sciences.

Together with architects RMJM, Turnberry advised the **University of Sheffield** on the preparation of a Comprehensive Development Framework for its estate across the city.

The final element is advice to **York Racecourse** on the possibilities of expansion of its activities having regard to the impending redevelopment of the nearby Terry's chocolate factory.

Index

architecture art design
fashion history photography
theory and things

www.bdpworld.com

black dog
publishing

© 2006 Black Dog Publishing Limited, the authors
and copyright holders

Text by The Duke of Devonshire, Professor Tim Wilson,
and Nadine Monem at Black Dog Publishing
Designed by Draught Associates

Black Dog Publishing Limited
Unit 4.4 Tea Building
56 Shoreditch High Street
London
E1 6JJ

Tel: +44 (0)20 7613 1922
Fax: +44 (0)20 7613 1944
Email: info@bdp.demon.co.uk

All opinions expressed within this publication are those of the authors
and not necessarily of the publisher.

British Library Cataloguing-in-Publication Data.

A CIP record for this book is available from the British Library.

ISBN-10: 1 904772 60 9
ISBN-13: 978 1 904772 60 6

Cover image: The Street and Auditorium at the University of
Hertfordshire's new de Havilland Campus. Architects: RMJM, 2003.